SPOOKY
Spooky Tennessee

Also in the Spooky Series by S. E. Schlosser and Paul G. Hoffman

Spooky Appalachia
Spooky California
Spooky Campfire Tales
Spooky Canada
Spooky Christmas
Spooky Colorado
Spooky Florida
Spooky Georgia
Spooky Great Lakes
Spooky Great Smokies
Spooky Indiana
Spooky Maryland
Spooky Massachusetts
Spooky Michigan
Spooky Montana
Spooky New England
Spooky New Jersey
Spooky New Orleans
Spooky New York
Spooky North Carolina
Spooky Ohio
Spooky Oregon
Spooky Pennsylvania
Spooky South
Spooky Southwest
Spooky Texas
Spooky Virginia
Spooky Washington
Spooky Wisconsin
Spooky Yellowstone

SPOOKY
Spooky Tennessee

Tales of Hauntings, Strange Happenings,
and Other Local Lore

RETOLD BY S. E. SCHLOSSER
ILLUSTRATED BY PAUL G. HOFFMAN

Globe Pequot
ESSEX, CONNECTICUT

Globe Pequot

An imprint of Globe Pequot, the trade division of
The Rowman & Littlefield Publishing Group, Inc.
4501 Forbes Blvd., Ste. 200
Lanham, MD 20706
www.rowman.com

Distributed by NATIONAL BOOK NETWORK

British Library Cataloguing in Publication Information available

Library of Congress Cataloging-in-Publication Data

Names: Schlosser, S. E., author. | Hoffman, Paul G., illustrator.
Title: Spooky Tennessee : tales of hauntings, strange happenings, and other
  local lore / retold by S.E. Schlosser ; illustrated by Paul G. Hoffman.
Description: Essex, Connecticut : Globe Pequot, 2024. | Includes
  bibliographical references.
Identifiers: LCCN 2023059593 (print) | LCCN 2023059594
  (ebook) | ISBN 9781493069927 (paperback) | ISBN 9781493069934
(epub)
Subjects: LCSH: Haunted places—Tennessee. | Ghost stories, American—
  Tennessee. | Folklore—Tennessee.
Classification: LCC BF1472.U6 S334 2024 (print) | LCC BF1472.U6
  (ebook) | DDC 133.109768—dc23/eng/20240216
LC record available at https://lccn.loc.gov/2023059593
LC ebook record available at https://lccn.loc.gov/2023059594

For my family: David, Dena, Tim, Arlene, Hannah,
Seth, Theo, Rory, Emma, Nathan, Ben, Karen,
Davey, Deb, Gabe, Clare, Jack, and Chris

For my friends: Jessica, Peter, Evelyn, Eleanor and Grace

For Sandy Laws and the staff at the Archives of
Appalachia. Thank you so much for your help.

For Greta Schmitz, Paul Hoffman, and the staff
at Globe Pequot. Thanks for all you do!

Contents

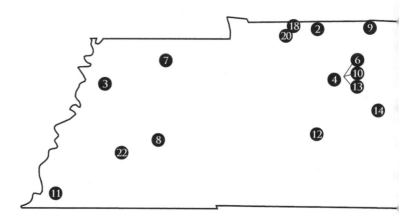

❶	Cookeville	❽	Jackson
❷	Adams	❾	Portland
❸	Dyersburg	❿	Nashville
❹	Belle Meade	⓫	Memphis
❺	Celina	⓬	Maury County
❻	Nashville	⓭	Nashville
❼	Weakley County	⓮	Rutherford County

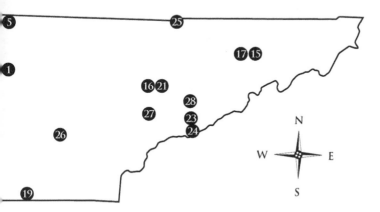

15 Carter County 22 Hatchie National Wildlife Refuge

16 Knoxville 23 Gatlinburg

17 Johnson City 24 Great Smoky Mountains

18 Clarksville 25 Cumberland Gap

19 Chattanooga 26 Rhea County

20 Montgomery County 27 Maryville

21 Knoxville 28 Sevier County

Introduction

I felt a frisson of anxiety pass through me as my friends and I joined the group gathering beside the visitor center. We had driven up to Adams, Tennessee, that morning to take a tour of the Bell Witch Cave, which was reported to house one of the state's most infamous spirits, and I was already on edge, disturbed by several prophetic dreams that had awakened me in the night. I had inherited some of the abilities of my psychic Pennsylvania Dutch great-grandfather, a famous faith healer, and my "sixth sense" had already informed me that this place had a seriously dark aura to it.

A replica of the original Bell house was our first stop. As we stepped onto the path that led toward the cave, a cold breeze sprang up around us and I could have sworn a voice was wailing in the wind. Folks around me were shivering and rubbing their arms reflexively, not a normal reaction on a warm Tennessee day. As soon as we left the path to cross a field toward the place where they'd built the replica house, the mysterious voice and breeze subsided.

Okay, *that* was spooky, I decided, quickening my pace. If things went south at any point during this tour, my plan was to run for the car!

As we explored the rooms in the replica cabin, the guide told the story of the Bell Witch haunting. It was sometime around 1817 when John Bell and his family first encountered the spirit. Strange animal sightings and unexplained noises gradually escalated to knocking on the walls and objects being moved around the house. Bedclothes were jerked off the inhabitants, hair was pulled, and other nasty tricks were played. A local pastor was invited to spend the night, and he received the same rough treatment. Afterward, he told the family their house was inhabited by a spirit, just like those in the Bible. The story spread around the community and farther, and many people came by the house to see the spirit in action (Old Hickory and the Bell Witch).

The spirit took pleasure in tormenting daughter Betsy Bell and her father, John Bell. One day the family returned home to find their father dead from poison. The Bell Witch claimed to have killed him. A few years later, the spirit plagued Betsy until she broke her engagement to a local lad of whom the spirit disapproved. The Bell Witch made several accurate prophetic predictions during its time with the family and promised to return at a future date. Folklore claims that the Bell Witch reemerged on the Bell property in a cave the family used for cold storage. It has remained in residence ever since.

I was shaking as we hiked down the steep riverside path leading to the Bell Witch Cave. The vibe of that area was very dark, and I had no doubt that the place was haunted. There was a brook flowing out of the cave entrance, which had vertical iron bars blocking it, with an open door in the center for visitors to walk through.

We were met at the end by a guide who pointed out some Native American burial sites in the bluff right above the cave. My queasy feeling returned as I stared up at them. Then we followed our guide through a narrow, low tunnel filled with stream water and river rocks. It opened into a broad room with several large niches on either side of the stream and a wide opening overhead on the right, above a flowstone.

I stumbled my way to a dry spot, feeling as if I was going to vomit. The room was so full of negative energy, it made my head swim. I hunched against the pain of it. The rest of the tour slowly gathered around me, finding places to stand on either side of the streambed. They gazed in fascination at the places where tribesmen had splintered out arrowheads and exclaimed at the small opening in the rocky ledge on the left side of the cave where they had found a small Native American girl buried, an apparent victim of the Trail of Tears. As the guide spoke of the little girl, some of my pain and dizziness ebbed. I straightened up, wondering if it was the girl's spirit I was feeling, and if the guide's acknowledgment had appeased the spirit I felt when I entered the room.

The group continued into a second, even narrower and lower tunnel; I stayed behind to pay my respects to the little girl's grave and keep an eye on one of my cavern-loving friends, who had lingered behind to study each formation in the room. When she was done with her inspection, we entered the second narrow tunnel. I took the lead, wading through the streambed, bent nearly double in places due to the low roof. There were many active formations in this second tunnel.

I paused to admire a small water cave in miniature and then stepped forward along the next leg of the tunnel. Suddenly I was shoved by an invisible force on my left. I slipped sideways and banged my head sharply against a rock in the tunnel ceiling overhead. The world went white for a moment. I gasped and braced myself against my knees, dizzy with shock. What had just happened?

Behind me, my friend exclaimed in fright. I told her I was alright, though I wasn't sure that was entirely true. Finding a stable place on the rocky floor, I took several breaths, clutching my bleeding scalp. Then I turned to look at my friend. She was studying the sharp rock that had "bitten" me. A large clump of my hair was wrapped around the point. She unwrapped it and put it into her pocket, not wanting to leave any bit of me in that strange, haunted place. I couldn't have agreed more.

I picked my way carefully through the rest of the tunnel and emerged into a second chamber. I scrambled up several boulders to the place the group had gathered and found a safe spot at the center of the crowd, hopefully far away from the shoving spirit of the tunnel. When we we're all assembled, the guide told us a few of the paranormal things that had happened in the cave, including people being touched by unseen hands, having their hair pulled, and voices coming from behind a flowstone that blocked the rest of the tunnel.

The spiritual energy in the cave was through the roof, I noted, rubbing my aching head. It was impacting several members of the group: Some giggled uncontrollably, others whispered in high-pitched voices, and one woman looked as if she was ready to throw up. *Right there with you*, I thought grimly. The guide quieted the group and asked us to listen for spirits. The murmur of voices from behind the stone rose swiftly, followed by a thumping sound—faint but distinct. Were those drums? The hairs on the back of my neck prickled and my knees started to shake.

Following this demonstration, the tour group's exodus from the cavern was rather hasty. We stopped for a few more photos but mostly concentrated on getting out. I had a moment of fright when we reached the first room. My formation-loving friend scrambled up a bunch of boulders to peer into an overhead opening that led to an upper chamber of the cave. It made my skin crawl just to look at the opening. The guide had told us a supernatural story that took place on the upper level. One of the Bell boys got trapped in a crawl space up there; a phantom light appeared in the chamber and yanked him to safety, pulling him down from the upper level and thrusting him out the entrance tunnel we had just used for our tour. He was afraid to tell his parents what happened, but the Bell Witch spilled the beans on him when he got home.

My sixth sense told me that this chamber was taboo. It was very haunted, and my friend shouldn't be standing there. I was not the only one she made nervous. Her sister made a joke about "beaming up" and begged her to come down. We both gave a sigh of relief when she reached the cavern floor unscathed.

I made good time trotting up the steep trail and out, out, out of that creepy cavern. I paused for a scant two minutes to buy some research books and then headed to the car. My friends, having learned what to do for a seriously spooked psychic based on previous adventures we'd had while researching folklore stories for *Spooky Tennessee*, fed me cashews and sparkling water to help me ground back to the present. We compared notes on our different cave experiences on the way home.

My friends patched up my head, which bore a three-inch cut from the sharp rock I hit when I was pushed in the tunnel, and then we reviewed the photos we took during the tour. We had captured multiple ghost lights throughout the cavern, and there were some crazy vortexes in my photos. Most frightening of all was the photo of my friend when she was staring into the upper chamber. In the picture she looked as if she was being drawn upward by a force field from above. Her feet had almost lifted off the ground; her eyes were glazed as if hypnotized and her nose had started to blur, as if she was flickering in and out of reality. The image was terrifying.

After seeing the photos, my friends decide this was their one and only visit to the Bell Witch Cave. Rubbing my sore skull with its bloody scratch, I agreed with them.

Happy Hauntings!

—Sandy Schlosser

PART ONE
Ghost Stories

1

The Chicken Thief

It was the coldest winter on record—at least in Cookeville—and something was stealing chickens right out of their henhouses. It was happening all over town. At first, folks thought a fox or raccoon was responsible, so they put locks on their coops to foil the crafty critters. But the locks didn't work. Chickens kept vanishing, night after night.

Folks started leaving their dogs in the yard overnight. It didn't help. The critter had obviously learned to wait until the dogs found a warm place to curl up against the winter cold before entering the chicken coops. A few families bought fancy critter traps and set them up near their henhouses, but after the mailman got caught in one of them and broke his arm, this practice was discontinued.

There was much debate over the identity of the chicken thief. Half the townsfolk believed the culprit was a very clever racoon; the other half believed a human was behind the thefts. Everyone was trying to solve the mystery before there were no more chickens left in Cookeville.

The correct answer was human, but the only person who knew that was the culprit. The chicken thief was a handyman

THE CHICKEN THIEF

who had arrived in town sometime in the fall and made his living doing odd jobs. When work dried up during the winter months, he turned to thieving to fill his empty belly. He spent daylight hours studying the local henhouses and chicken coops for flaws and weaknesses, of which he found plenty. Most of the local chicken coops were built of logs with wide cracks between them. The chicken thief could look through the gaps and see the birds all fluffed up against the winter cold as they perched on the long poles set up for roosting. A clever thief could reach in and grab a bird or two without anyone being the wiser, he reckoned. But the birds were not inclined to linger near the chilly drafts coming through the walls. They huddled together in the warmest spot in the coop, which was typically too far for the chicken thief to reach.

He pondered the matter for several days as his food stores grew slim and his belly became one long, hungry rumble. Then he came up with a clever idea he thought might work. The chicken thief went into the woods and selected a long branch about the size of a typical roosting pole, and he warmed the branch up near the fire until the pine resin melted out. Then he made his way to the nearest henhouse and slipped the pole through a crack in the logs right next to the roost where the hens huddled together, half frozen with the cold. When the chickens felt the heat coming off the pine pole, they raised their heads and started clucking at one another. The heat felt so good on their chilly feet that they stepped onto the new pole to warm themselves. After a few minutes the chickens tucked their heads under their wings and closed their eyes to sleep. And that's when the thief struck. He pulled the pine pole back toward the wall until he could reach the closest hen, then he grabbed it and dropped it into his sack before it knew what was happening. By the time the other chickens got to squawking, the thief was long gone down the trail to his little old cabin back in the woods.

The heated pole method of chicken thievery worked every time. On really cold nights, the thief could secure two or even three fat hens at one time, which provided him with food for several days.

Now there was one house—the biggest in the settlement—that was a favorite of the chicken thief because a huge flock of fat hens was always clucking around the barnyard. An elderly widow lived in that house, and those chickens were her pride and joy. Each morning when she went to feed her flock, she'd count them, and every time a chicken went missing, she'd search the whole farm for it. The widow was the first person in the settlement to put a lock on her henhouse, and she was furious when her prize chickens kept vanishing despite her precautions. One night she set up camp in the chicken coop, a rifle lying across her knees, hoping to shoot the varmint that was stealing her prized hens.

The chicken thief 'bout had a heart attack when he peeked through the logs of the henhouse that night and saw the widow sitting there. He was sure she had him, for his peephole was right next to the log where she'd set herself down for the night. But the widow's eyes were fixed on the roosting hens huddled against the far wall, so she missed the moment he looked through the peephole.

The chicken thief crept away mighty quick, crawling on hands and knees until he was sure he hadn't been seen. Then he hightailed it down the road and back to his little house, his heart beating so fast he thought it would bang out of his chest.

He went hungry that night and avoided the widow's house for a couple of days.

At church that Sunday, the chicken thief learned that the old widow had caught pneumonia after spending a cold night in the henhouse and had passed away soon after. The funeral was being held that very afternoon because the family wanted to bury her before the approaching snowstorm froze the ground solid.

When the widow's eldest son—who had inherited the property—announced that he was heading back to Knoxville directly after the funeral to pack up his family and belongings for the move to Cookeville, the chicken thief started planning a raid on the dead widow's henhouse. The family wouldn't get there until Monday or Tuesday, he reckoned, which left him plenty of time to fill his sack with enough delicious fat hens to last him the rest of the winter.

When darkness fell, the chicken thief crept into the yard with his hot pine pole and poked it through a large crack near the cold roost where the fat hens huddled in sleep. After a few moments, he felt a weight settling onto the pole; he grinned to himself, envisioning fat hens stepping onto the warm stick, one after another. The pole grew heavier and heavier. The thief was overjoyed, for he reckoned he'd attracted one of the fattest hens in the coop, or maybe even one of the big turkeys that sometimes joined them in the roost.

Breathless with anticipation, the thief carefully pulled the pole back through the hole until he could reach through and grab the fat fowl with his hands. His hand closed over something huge! It was the size of a prize-winning turkey and was extremely cold to his touch. No wonder it had settled on his hot pole.

The chicken thief wondered how he was going to squeeze such a large bird through the crack in the logs. It seemed impossible, but he wasn't going to let go of his prize. He held tight while the bird kicked and fluttered and fought in his grasp. He tightened his grip and used his free hand to wrap the bag around it like a rope. Then he braced both feet against the henhouse and tugged for all he was worth until he was almost flat on his back.

He felt something give way, and the logs cracked open with a loud bang. The chicken thief fell backward, crashing onto the ground with a huge white object sprawled across his chest.

When the chicken thief took a good look at the thing lying on top of him, a thrill of horror raced up his spine. It resembled a corpse, for it was wrapped head to toe in a white winding sheet that was stained with dirt. He shifted, trying to wriggle out from underneath the grisly object, and found himself staring into the wide dead eyes of the recently deceased widow! She had clawed herself out of her buried coffin and set herself down in the henhouse with her old rifle cradled against her chest to guard her prized hens until her son returned with his family.

The chicken thief screamed so loud it startled all the birds in the henhouse. He rolled out from under the corpse, leapt to his feet, and levitated over the nearest fence, accompanied by the terrified squawking of the hens. He kept on running right through the settlement and down the road toward Nashville. And for all I know, he might have kept on running even farther than that. Anyway, he was never seen in Cookeville again.

The eldest son found his mother's corpse lying outside the henhouse when he arrived with his family on Tuesday morning. It was a terrible scandal. No one knew who had vandalized the widow's grave, and it caused much speculation among the settlers in the area. They never made the connection between the grave robber and the chicken thief. At least, not until now.

2

Old Hickory and the Bell Witch

ADAMS

"I warn you, Sally-girl," Granny said to me one hot summer afternoon as we sat on the front porch drinking ice-cold glasses of homemade lemonade, "there are probably a hundred different versions of the Bell Witch story floating around the country. All I can tell you about the Bell Witch is the story as it was told to me by my great granddaddy. If you want 'truth' and 'facts,' you would do better to read one of the books that have been written about the Bell Witch."

"I would like to hear your story," I said promptly, bouncing a bit in my chair from pure excitement. Granny gave me a look that told me she did not consider my behavior up to the standards of a Southern lady. I sat still.

"The Bell family," Granny began, "moved to Robertson County sometime around 1804. They were a God-fearing family who were leading members of the community. The spirit that plagued the Bell family first made its presence known in 1817. According to my great-granddaddy, the spirit commenced its activities by rapping on the walls of the house. Shortly thereafter, it began pulling the quilts off the children's beds, tugging on their hair, and slapping and pinching them

OLD HICKORY AND THE BELL WITCH

until red marks appeared on their faces and bodies. It would steal sugar right out of the bowl, spill the milk, and taunt the Bell family by laughing and cursing at them. Really, it was quite a rude spirit!" Granny paused to give her opinion. She took a dainty sip of lemonade and continued her story.

"Naturally, all this hullabaloo caused great excitement throughout the community. People would come from miles around to meet this spirit, which would gossip with them and curse at them and play tricks on them. According to my great-granddaddy, John Bell and his family would feed and entertain all these guests at their own expense—not an easy task. The house would get so full that people were forced to camp outside.

"When Old Hickory heard about the Bell Witch, he decided to pay a visit to the Bell home. The general brought a party up with him from Nashville. To avoid discomforting the Bell family, they filled a wagon with provisions and tents for camping out.

"General Jackson and his party approached the plantation, laughing and talking about the spirit and all its pranks. The men were on horseback, following the wagon with their supplies. They were boasting of how they would best the Bell Witch when suddenly the wagon stopped short. Tug and pull as they might, the horses could not move the wagon an inch, even though they were on flat ground with no trace of mud. The driver shouted and snapped the whip, but the horses could not shift the wagon. General Jackson asked all the horsemen to dismount, and together they pushed against the wagon, to no avail. The wagon would not budge.

"Old Hickory had the men examine the wheels one by one—taking them off, checking the axles, and then reattaching them. There was nothing wrong with the wheels. They tried to move the wagon again, whipping up the horses, shouting and pushing. But still the wagon would not budge. The men were completely flummoxed. What was going on? Then the general shouted, 'Boys, it's the witch!'

"An eerie voice answered Old Hickory from the shrubbery: 'All right, General. Let the wagon move on. I will see you again tonight.'

"The men looked around in astonishment, for they had seen no one nearby. At once, the horses started moving without any prompting from the coachman, and the wagon rumbled along the road as if it had never been stuck at all.

"Old Hickory and his men were sobered by their strange experience. Suddenly the idea of camping out was not very appealing, even though one of their men was supposed to be a professional witch tamer.

"When the general's party reached the house, John Bell and his wife extended every courtesy to their distinguished guest and his friends, offering them food, drink, entertainment, and quarters for the night. But Old Hickory had only one entertainment in mind. He had come for witch hunting, and nothing else would do. After dining with the Bells, the whole party sat waiting for the spirit to appear. To while away the time, they listened to the boasts of the witch tamer, who had a gun with a silver bullet that he meant for the spirit. The men were secretly amused by the man's vanity, yet they found his presence oddly comforting after their strange experiences with the wagon. Here was someone who could handle the spirit.

"The hour grew late. Old Hickory was restless, and the men were getting drowsy. The witch tamer began taunting the spirit and playing with his gun. Suddenly there was the sound of footsteps crossing the floor. Everyone snapped to attention. Then the same eerie voice they had heard on the road exclaimed, 'I am here. Now shoot me!'

"The witch tamer aimed his gun at the place where they had heard the voice. He pulled the trigger, but the gun didn't fire. The spirit began to taunt him as the witch tamer tried to shoot the gun again. Then the spirit said, 'Now it's my turn.'

"Everyone heard the sounds of the witch tamer being slapped silly as he shouted, 'Lordy, Lordy!' and 'My nose!' and 'The devil's got me!' He began to dance about the parlor, screaming that the spirit was pricking him with pins and beating him. Then the door swung open of its own accord and the witch tamer raced outside, still shouting 'Lordy, Lordy!' as he ran down the lane. Everyone followed him outside, expecting him to drop dead, but aside from an occasional jump, twist, or shout, the witch tamer seemed likely to live. They watched him as he ran out of sight, while Old Hickory laughed until his sides were sore.

"They were all startled when they heard the spirit's voice among them again. It was laughing at its triumph over the witch tamer and claimed that there was another fraud in the group that it would expose the next night. The men were pretty shaken up when they heard the spirit's words. It was one thing to laugh at a fake witch tamer who got his comeuppance. It was quite another thing to realize that one of them might be the next target. Old Hickory was all set to stay a full week with the Bells, but his men were not so enthusiastic.

"My great-granddaddy didn't know exactly what happened that night to change Old Hickory's mind. Maybe the spirit played some pranks on him; maybe the justifiable fear of his men persuaded him. Whatever the case, General Andrew Jackson was up and away the next morning. By dark, Old Hickory's party had already reached Springfield, and they went on to Nashville the next day. Much later, Old Hickory was heard to remark, 'I'd rather fight the entire British Army than deal with the Bell Witch.'"

Granny took a sip of her lemonade and shook her head. "I don't blame the general one bit for leaving so quickly. I would have done the same thing."

"What happened to the Bell Witch?" I asked.

"Oh, most of the stories agree that the Bell Witch got worse and worse, tormenting Betsy Bell something awful and finally poisoning John Bell so that he died. They say the spirit laughed and sang in triumph at John's funeral. The spirit stayed for several months following the death of John Bell, putting pressure on Betsy to break her engagement with a man named Gardener, which Betsy did sometime around Easter of 1821. After that, the spirit told Mrs. Bell that it was going away but would visit again in seven years."

"Did it come back?" I asked.

"Yes, the spirit did return to visit the family seven years later, just as it promised," said Granny. "For about three weeks, the spirit talked with John Bell Jr., making predictions about the future, and promising to return in 107 years. As far as I know, the Bell family did not receive the second promised visit. I have heard some people claim that the Bell Witch never really left the Bells' property but still haunts the land to this day. I myself have not gone there to find out if this is true."

Granny finished her lemonade and peered at me from under the rim of her straw hat. "Well, Sally-girl, that's enough about evil spirits for one day. I am going back to my garden. Get along with you now. And don't forget those tomatoes I set aside for your mama."

"Yes, ma'am," I said meekly, taking my glass back to the kitchen before I started for home.

3

Incident at the Inn

I did a lot of traveling for my business back in the 1840s, and in those days it was no easy task. I relied on steamboats, horses, and carriages to get from place to place, and I always carried my money and my pistols belted around my waist.

One summer evening, I was traveling by steamboat up to Kentucky for a land sale when the engine developed a mechanical problem and the passengers were forced to offload while the boat was repaired.

It was clear that we would miss the land sale if we waited on the steamboat, so my business partner and I arranged to rent a carriage the following morning and then retired to a local inn for the night.

We ordered dinner and sat in the main dining room to eat it. As the evening progressed, the attitude of the innkeeper made me uneasy. He asked prying questions and exchanged sly glances with some of his regular patrons. Between us, my partner and I carried a sum in excess of five thousand dollars in cash. It was not a great leap of logic to determine that one or more of these individuals would be happy to relieve us of the contents of our money belts, and possibly our lives as well.

INCIDENT AT THE INN

My business partner and I decided that, for safety's sake, we would share a bedroom that night. After eating a greasy dinner that turned my stomach rather than filling it, we went upstairs to sleep.

The bedroom was built from rough log walls. There was no fireplace, only a single door and two tiny windows that were nailed shut in their frames. We spent the next several minutes taking precautions against being robbed and murdered. I checked for a trapdoor in the bare floor. There was none. My business partner tapped the walls, looking for hidden passages, and we both inspected the ceiling but deemed it solid. The only way in or out was the door, which we barred securely. We each took one side of the bed and went to sleep with our money belts under our pillows and cocked pistols at hand.

Around 2:00 a.m., I woke with a pounding heart as two big, sinewy hands closed around my neck, strangling the air out of me. A heavy figure was kneeling on my chest, and I instinctively grabbed the arms of my assailant, trying to pry his hands off my throat. I realized that the figure was completely naked and covered with strangely long hair.

We grappled fiercely in silence for several desperate moments. I knew that if I did not subdue him quickly, the lack of air would kill me. In a frantic bid for life, I pushed myself upright, forcing the figure backward, and used my momentum to cast my assailant violently away. He fell upon the wooden floor with a loud banging sound, which jarred my business partner awake.

"What is that? What's happening?" my colleague called in dismay.

"Thieves! Stranglers," I choked out, my voice raspy from the bruises on my throat. "Light the lantern before we are murdered!"

My business partner fumbled with the matches and, a moment later, held the lantern up to survey the room. No one was there.

I was shocked. Where had my assailant gone? I'd heard the boards thump when I flung him off the bed, but the floor was empty. The door was still barred, the nailed windows untouched, and there was no crack in the walls that would admit a creature larger than a mouse.

I touched my sore throat, wondering if I'd had a bad dream. But my companion's eyes rounded until they resembled large saucers, and he exclaimed in horror.

"What do you see?" I demanded.

"There are red marks all around your neck. It looks as if a man with very large hands tried to strangle you," he exclaimed.

"That's what it felt like," I agreed, and told him exactly what I'd felt, heard, and seen.

He poured me some water to drink from the pitcher by the bedside and made me drink every drop. It soothed a bit of the ache, but the injury was severe enough that I knew it would take several days for my voice to heal.

Neither one of us was inclined to sleep anymore that night. Not when a violent and hairy stranger could so easily appear and vanish again from our small chamber. We got dressed and sat up the rest of the night with our money belts around our waists and a finger on the hammer of our pistols.

"Do you think it was a ghost?" my business partner asked once, around 5:00 a.m., as we waited for the sun to rise.

"Or a demon," I said grimly. "I have no idea what else it *could* be."

"I wonder what happened to cause such a dark creature to haunt this place," my colleague mused.

I didn't respond. I was too anxious and sore to care.

My hairy assailant did not return, thank Providence, and we left the inn as soon as day broke.

We reached the land sale with time to spare and turned in our rented carriage. Within two weeks our business in Kentucky was swiftly and satisfactorily concluded, so we made our way home on the steamboat as planned. While we were aboard, we struck up an acquaintance with a passenger who boarded the vessel in Dyersburg. When we asked for the latest news, he grew quite excited and said, "We have an unsolved mystery in Dyersburg."

"What mystery is that?" I asked, leaning back in my seat and taking a sip of ale.

"It's a nine days' wonder," he said earnestly. "A traveler was found strangled to death in one of the upstairs bedrooms of a local inn. The innkeeper found him lying dead on the floor with cruel black marks around his throat. But no one knows who did the deed or how it was accomplished, because the door to his room was barred from the inside and they had to break it down to enter!"

4

Dutchman's Curve

BELLE MEADE

I was working as a general assistant at a local train station in the days following the First World War, and I was determined to make a name for myself in the railroading business. I had taken a demanding job with the promise of promotion if I stuck to it, which didn't leave me with much time off. When my supervisor gave me three days' leave as a bonus for a job well done, I jumped at the opportunity to visit my brother and his wife, who lived on the far side of the state, just a few miles out of Memphis.

DUTCHMAN'S CURVE

I sent a telegram to my folks telling them I was on the way and boarded the first westbound train available. I got off at my brother's small station late in the evening and hoofed it a couple of miles down the road to my brother's house. When I got there, I found the house dark and the yard silent. I was surprised, for I expected my brother to wait up for me. I hammered on the doors to see if I could wake my brother and his missus, but no one answered.

I finally realized that no one was home. It looked as if they hadn't received the telegram saying I was coming to stay and had gone away to tend to some business. I thought about breaking a window and letting myself into the house, but I knew my sister-in-law would be sore at me if I did. So I decided to head back to the train station. I'd missed the sleeper train back to Nashville and there wasn't another train scheduled until the morning, but I could let myself into one of the sheds and get a few hours' sleep in relative warmth before catching the first train home in the morning.

It was almost midnight when I reached the station. I was tired, hungry, and mentally cussing out my brother for not being home, alternating with cussing myself out for taking a trip to see family when I could have been sleeping in my own bed.

I was just making myself comfortable in a rough old storage shed when I heard the rumble of a train passing through the station. I sat up in surprise, wondering what the heck was happening. It was part of my duties to know the timing of every vehicle on the track, and I knew there were no more trains scheduled on this local line until morning. I heard the grinding of the brakes and the telltale release of steam. The unscheduled train had halted a few yards down the track heading toward Nashville.

I grabbed my overnight bag and stepped outside to see what was going on. About fifty yards down the line, I saw a steam train standing next to a water butt and realized that the engineer must be taking on water. I didn't recognize the train, which was odd. It was an older model and looked a little battered in the dim light of the crescent moon. It was pulling several of the wooden passenger cars that our line was slowly phasing out, along with several Pullman sleeper cars.

As I walked toward the mysterious train, the wheels started moving again and it pulled away from the water butt. I picked up the pace and reached the track in time to swing myself up onto the rear platform of the last sleeper car. With any luck, one of the beds would be empty and I could get a good night's sleep after all. I just hoped the porter wouldn't give me a hard time because I'd boarded the train between stops.

The door to the sleeper car was stuck. I had to put my shoulder to it and give it a hard shove to get it open. I frowned. Someone should have fixed that before letting the car leave the train depot. That was bad management.

The sleeper car was lit by a single lantern and there was no one inside, which was so very strange that it gave me goosebumps along my arms. At the very least, I'd expected the porter to be standing in front of the door, demanding the cost of the ticket from me plus a big tip for the inconvenience of making up another berth.

As I walked through the car, I saw that the beds were unmade and many of the fittings were askew, as if all the passengers had left the train in a rush at the last stop and the porter hadn't come round yet to prepare the car for new riders. The smell of fire and coal smoke was much stronger than it would normally be for a car this far from the engine. I left the back door open and went to open the front door as well to help clear the air.

I picked a berth at random and set about fixing the disarray enough to sleep. The bedclothes had picked up the burning smell and the sheets felt gritty in my hands, as if ash had been strewn over them. The inside of the small room was colder than the air outside, which didn't seem possible. It was an eerie sensation, breathing in the smell of fire while feeling ice cold. I dropped the bedclothes and stumbled back into the corridor with my overnight bag, unwilling to spend another moment in the berth. I'd find another one.

But they were all the same—cold and gritty and smelling strongly of smoke. And the windows were so blackened with ash you couldn't see outside. It was uncanny.

To make matters worse, the train had picked up speed and was now running at a rate of speed that was unsafe, to say the least. Everything was shaking and rolling and jumping so much that I had to drop my overnight bag and hold on with both hands to stay upright. The engineer must be crazy or drunk to take such risks. Maybe that was why there were no passengers aboard. They'd all bailed out at the last station to get away from the madness.

To tell you the truth, by this time I was wishing I could leave the train myself. I wasn't fond of jumping, but the thought of staying aboard had little appeal. Then I remembered the bell cord. I would pull it and stop the train! If the conductor came, I'd tell him that I worked for the railroad and would report him and the engineer for running the train in such a dangerous manner if they didn't mend matters immediately.

I stumbled and rolled my way to the bell pull, hanging on for dear life whenever we went around a bend. When I reached it, I grabbed hold and gave it a tug. The darned thing broke in my hand. I looked down at it in astonishment and saw that the cord was blackened and damaged, as if it had been too near a fire or hit by burning ash. This was terrible negligence. No passenger car should be allowed to run with damaged equipment. It wasn't safe. I rolled up the cord and put it into my pocket to offer as proof when I gave my report to my supervisor.

The train was still barreling ahead at full speed. It leaned so hard at the bends that the wheels nearly came off the track. The entire train shook when they crashed back down onto the rails. I ducked into the front berth, ignoring the shocking cold and the pungent odor of smoke, and held on for dear life while I pondered the folly of trying to walk through the passenger cars to the front to confront the engineer. That seemed like a death sentence. Then I thought of the brake. I could pull the brake on the Pullman car; the engineer should feel the drag and stop the train, unless he was an utter fool, which—given current circumstances—was a possibility I couldn't ignore. Still, it was the best I could do for me and whatever passengers were still aboard this wretched vehicle.

I staggered my way onto the platform, holding on for all I was worth, and got hold of the brake wheel. I jammed it down as hard as I could. To my horror, the brake chain snapped as easily as the bell cord. This train was a dilapidated wreck. It should not be in service!

I crawled back into the sleeper car, on the theory that it was slightly safer to be inside, and tried to decide if there was anything else I could do to avoid jumping from a train going fifty miles an hour. I crouched inside the small washroom since it was slightly less smelly in there and tried to think through my terror. Slowly, it dawned on me that the train was racing through every crossing and station without stopping or sounding its whistle. Had the engineer dropped dead in the cab? Was that why the train was running with such abandon? But the fireman should have stepped up and stopped the train if the engineer died. What was going on?

I had no idea how long I had been aboard this nightmare train. It felt like forever. We could be fifty miles from Nashville or right around the corner; I could not tell with the ash-covered windows. I caught up my bag and slowly crept my way through the rattling, swaying, rolling passage to the rear platform where I'd first entered the train. The door had slammed shut at the first bend, but I hauled it open again, bracing myself and leaning back so far, I almost fell when it swung wide. I crawled out onto the platform, shaking like the proverbial leaf because I was so frightened. Where was I?

It was that funny time between dark and day, and I was still trying to identify the scenery flashing past my tired eyes when I heard the almighty crash of two engines smashing into each other at full speed somewhere just ahead. The platform lurched beneath me, and then the entire train vanished as suddenly as it had appeared just a few hours ago. I was thrown into a small grove of trees growing along the tracks and rolled several yards before my head cracked down on a stone—and the world went dark.

When I awoke, it was full daylight and I was lying in the dirt and gravel beside a stream. A brief examination told me my skull was still intact and no bones were broken, so I picked myself up, and then groaned when I realized I'd have to stoop over again to pick up my overnight bag, which was lying a few feet away. I made my way along a likely looking path toward the sound of a road and discovered myself to be in Belle Meade, only a few miles from my home.

Maybe I'd gotten drunk after work yesterday, passed out by the stream, and dreamed the whole gosh-dang thing, I mused as I walked wearily home. That made more sense than a crazy ride across state on a vanishing train.

I didn't realize until I stepped into my little house that my clothes reeked of smoke and my hands were covered with ash. I reached into my pocket and my trembling fingers closed on the burnt bell cord. I pulled it out and stared at it. Then I looked up at the kitchen calendar hanging on the wall and saw the date. It was July 9, 1928. Exactly ten years ago, the No. 1 express train out of Memphis had collided with the No. 4 train out of Nashville, killing 101 people. Called the worst train crash in American history, it had happened at Dutchman's Curve in Belle Meade—the exact location in which I found myself this morning after a harrowing ride on a vanishing train.

I gasped and my knees gave way. I dropped to the floor, panting and wringing my hands in shock as I realized the truth. I'd just hitched a ride on a ghost train.

5

Skull House

Folks in town were mighty surprised when a red-bearded stranger made a cash bid on the old farmhouse near the place of the skulls. It was owned by a well-to-do landowner in Celina, but no one wanted it on account of the Native American burial ground that stood beside it. You'd have to be desperate or foolish to live in a place so full of haunts.

Local legend said a mighty battle was waged between the Creek and Choctaw on that spot long before European settlers set foot on the land. The Creek were badly outnumbered, and bodies were strewn all over the riverbank when a small band of warriors retreated to a cave high on the face of the river bluff. The cavern could only be reached by pole ladders, which they pulled up as soon as the refuge was attained, and they kept the besieging enemy at bay with arrows and fragments of rock. The Choctaw settled down near the bluff to wait. The cave had no known exit, so it would not be long before hunger drove the last of the Creek warriors into their grasp.

For the next several days, the warriors explored the caverns, seeking a way out. Finally, a young Creek chief discovered an outlet a mile from the cliff entrance. He brought the hungry

SKULL HOUSE

men a rabbit he had slain—the first meal they'd eaten in almost a week. Then, at moonrise, he led them through a devious underground pathway to the second entrance. The Creek warriors emerged victorious from the cave, certain they had outwitted their enemies. But a sudden movement in the shadows alerted them to the presence of the Choctaw, who had observed the young chief disappearing into the hidden second entrance and had laid a trap for the survivors. The final skirmish was swiftly over. The Creek were marched back to camp, where they were put to death the next day. The smoke from the pyre could be seen for miles as the Choctaw victors broke camp and went on their way. They left behind the skeletons and the beads, shells, and pottery of the defeated, as well as any treasures the Creek warriors had left behind in the cavern.

The ancient battle was so fierce that there were still skulls aplenty to be found in the riverbank for years to come, and it was rumored that the ghosts of the Creek warriors roamed the riverside and haunted the old farmhouse that bordered it. Anyhow, no one who rented the place ever stayed there long, and the owner finally gave up and let it go to ruin.

So when the red-bearded bloke stopped at the mercantile to ask to be directed to the owner of the old farmhouse, it caused quite a stir.

"What do you want that old place for? It's haunted, don't you know. There's plenty of nice houses you could buy on this side of town," old Uncle Wallis opined.

"Name's Jeremiah, and I'm starting up a business," the red-bearded fellow replied. "I've been asked to plant a truck garden to support folks in the new settlement. I can't afford to buy one of your fancy houses until my business succeeds."

"Hit's your funeral," Uncle Wallis said. He spat in in the rain barrel and then gave him the directions to the wealthy landowner's place.

A week later, the new owner of Skull Farm, as the locals jokingly dubbed it, drove through town with a wagonload of mattocks and picks and shovels, enough to make a large truck garden and then some. This was a sure sign of his industry, the locals reckoned. Come spring, his new truck garden was sure to be a success.

On the night of the full moon in October—more than a month after he sold Skull House to Jeremiah—the wealthy landowner was awakened by the sound of fearful yells and cries that made his hair stand on end. While his wife hid under the bedclothes, thinking their house was under attack, he ran outside to investigate. Two possum hunters, who had been heading home with their catch, came running into the yard to see if he needed help.

The three men hurried in the direction of Skull House, rifles at the ready, looking every which way for the source of the yelling. They found Jeremiah inside the old farmhouse, huddled in the chimney corner. He had been beaten black and blue. His face and hands were covered with scratches and sharp cuts, and his clothes were ripped in so many places they were about to fall off.

"Who did this to you?" cried the landowner. "We will summon the sheriff and have him arrested at once."

"T'aint anyone you can arrest," Jeremiah said sheepishly. He rubbed his hand over his face in embarrassment, and then told them his story.

"Six months ago I was plowing my little corn patch," he began, "when I looked up and saw this weather-beaten old man looking at me. He was wearing one of them old buckskin hunting shirts and held an old rifle in his hand. Looked like a cousin of Davy Crockett from out of the history books. Suddenly I realized that I could see the stalks of corn right through his body, and I knew it was a ghost."

The landowner gasped and exchanged glances with the possum hunters. Could it be possible?

"Turned out, the hant was my great-grandsire. He told me about a big jar full of gold beads and bracelets and nuggets the warriors had buried with one of their great leaders who died on the battlefield beside this here farm. He found it by accident one day when he was digging around the riverbank and barely escaped with his life, since the hants that guard the treasure try to kill anyone who gets anywhere near it.

"Once he went on to his reward, my great-grandsire found out that there was one night each year when the spirits were called away to a higher spiritual duty. During the full moon in October, the ghosts of the fallen warriors gathered for the great Corn Dance. From sundown of that night until the time the trees throw shadows over the place where it was buried, the jar is unguarded. My great-grandsire told me to buy this house—which was dirt cheap—and gave me directions to the burial site of the jar. Things have changed a might since he was alive, but I finally located the place where the gold rests, and I've been waiting ever since for the night of the full moon so I could retrieve it."

"Tonight's the night of the full moon," observed one of the possum hunters. "So where's the gold?"

"It's still in the gosh-dang hole," groaned Jeremiah. "I started digging around sundown, but that ground was hard as rock, and by midnight I was deeper than my head when I finally reached the jar. I was digging careful-like, 'cause my great-grandsire said it was lying on its side and there was plenty of gold dust in the bottom that would fall out if I broke it. So I scraped away handholds on each side and then straightened up for a moment to catch my breath. And that's when I realized the tree shadows had lengthened until they were covering the top of the hole."

He grimaced in remembered chagrin and said, "My time was up, and the jar of gold was still in the ground! I wasn't about to let all that work go to waste. I ducked down quick and scooped the jar up willy-nilly. Who cared if I lost a little gold dust? I'd still have the rest of the treasure. That jar was real heavy. I could tell I'd be a rich man if I made it out of that hole alive. I tossed the jar onto the riverbank and scrambled after it, but before I could jump out of the hole, someone banged me on the head with a war club. Then another club caught me on the ear, and another hit me on the shoulder. The warriors had returned from the Corn Dance and caught me with the treasure."

Jeremiah clutched his head as if it pained him and moaned. "There was more 'n fifty of them hants, all of them glowing with an eerie blue light. They had tomahawks and knives and bows and whatnot. All of them aimed at me! Arrows started flying every which way, as thick as raindrops, and I knew I had to get out of that hole or I was a dead man. I vaulted out of there quicker than a coon chased by hound dogs and raced for home. The hants followed me all the way across the burial ground, beating on me with their clubs while their thrown knives and arrows took pieces out of my clothes until I was half naked. It wasn't until I crossed the line between the old battlefield and my house that they vanished. I've been right here ever since."

One of the possum hunters dug into his pocket and handed Jeremiah the whiskey flask he carried to keep out the cold. The so-called truck gardener took it with shaking hands and drank deeply.

"Sunup's in another hour," said the landowner. "I reckon it will be safe then to check things out."

The other men agreed.

When daylight had firm hold of the farmyard, the men followed Jeremiah along the riverbank until they came to a deep, freshly dug hole with a round cavity at the bottom, exactly the shape of an old jar. There was no sign of the vessel on the riverbank or beneath the adjoining shrubbery. But in the loose earth beside the hole, there were several moccasin footprints, and an arrow was embedded in the tree behind it. The carnelian arrowhead looked as if it was freshly chipped.

"They've taken the jar with them," Jeremiah said mournfully. "We'll never find it now."

"Friend, I don't think it's safe for you to linger here," said one of the possum hunters nervously, staring at the arrow in the tree. "Them hants could be back at any time."

As he spoke, phantom drums began beating in the woods around them, echoing off the bluffs and chilling their bones. The men fled the battlefield so fast they left their hats behind. They had Jeremiah's wagon packed up within the hour, and the truck gardener went off to seek his fortune as far away from a Native American battleground as a fellow could get.

Skull House lay abandoned for several years after this incident. It finally burnt to the ground in a thunderstorm. Everyone thought it was good riddance.

6

At the General's House

The parking lot wasn't crowded when we reached the Hermitage, so my friends and I were first in line for tickets. The kids were excited for our walk around the grounds of the presidential mansion and kept asking questions as they strolled with their parents through the museum exhibits on their way to the entrance to the grounds.

I lagged behind. This was my first visit to President Andrew Jackson's home, and I eagerly drank in each sign, reading about the War of 1812 and Jackson's presidential races. Some of the themes were an eerie parallel to the present political situation, which gave me pause. The more things change, the more they stayed the same? Maybe.

I set the thought aside as I joined my friend outside the museum. We strolled up the lane toward the Hermitage house and its formal garden. The kids darted back and forth along the lane, fascinated by benches and tree stumps, wide lawns, and pastures with grazing horses. In between the chatter, my friend and I read informational signs and discussed the probable layout of house, land, and carriage drive, trying to reconcile old newspaper accounts with the scene before us. The Greek Revival

35

At the General's House

mansion was the fourth iteration of the house and looked lovely in the soft morning sunlight.

The house tour didn't start for an hour, so we guided the kids over to the formal gardens. They trotted ahead, chased by their patient father while my friend and I lingered over the flower beds, naming the herbs and blooms we recognized and debating the origins of others.

It wasn't until we rounded a corner and stood facing the family cemetery that a familiar chill ran up my arms. I stopped in my tracks, realizing that someone unseen was watching us. My friend was called away by her family, so I proceeded alone toward the tombstones, glancing at names and dates, sending a small burst of light and hope as a prayer for those who had gone before. All the while, I felt eyes upon me.

I turned and looked at the presidential tomb, which lay beneath a small Greek-style temple designed by Morrison. Standing between two columns, one hand pressed against the top of a cane, was a tall, gaunt man holding himself ramrod straight as if he was in the military. He had bushy gray hair above a long thin face, and his blue eyes looked straight into mine.

I gave the General a small bow and he gave me a brisk nod. Old Hickory held a cigar in his free hand, and the smell of its smoke made my nostrils twitch. Nodding toward the grave of his wife, I extended my condolences. His face softened, and he thanked me. Then he told me about the garden around us, which she had loved, and bade me read the inscription on her tombstone. The tribute to his wife was moving, and so I told him. The General swallowed, eyes bright, and told me to keep my eyes open for Rachel as I continued my stroll. Sometimes she walked about the grounds of her former home.

A school group came upon us then, interrupting the conversation, and Old Hickory vanished as abruptly as he had appeared. A moment later, my friend and children reappeared with exciting news on the flower front. They'd found some larkspur that was positively magical in appearance. I smiled and followed them up the path.

The hour passed quickly. Soon it was time for the kids and their father to head home for a birthday party while my friend and I queued up for the house tour.

I saw the ghost watching from the curve in the elliptical staircase to the second floor as soon as I stepped through the door. Her eyes were kind, but there was a stubborn tilt to her chin and an air of authority about her, as if she was the guardian of this mansion and we were intruders in her domain.

I turned my attention to the docent's lecture, peering around at the printed scenic wallpaper in the massive entry hall, and then peered into each room in turn as he described its purpose and contents. The next time I glanced at the staircase, the ghost was no longer visible. But I could still feel her watching us.

Our tour continued through the main bedrooms, the two offices, and then upstairs to the children's bedrooms and the guest rooms. It wasn't until the official end of the guided portion that I realized that the next stage of the tour led down the elliptical staircase and then out through the back entrance to the self-guided portion of the tour. I swallowed hard, goose bumps breaking out all over my skin. I couldn't see the spirit on the staircase but, boy, could I feel her. She was watching over the General's house, and she refused to move from her chosen post. I gulped and gestured for my friend to proceed me down the staircase. Then I carefully began my descent, knowing the ghost was waiting at the curve.

As soon as my friend passed her, the ghost stepped to the center of the staircase and blocked my path. In that moment, I realized that the spirit wanted me to acknowledge her role in the General's house. She was the one who watched over this home. Anyone who entered this place needed to go through her. I gulped, realizing that she meant that literally. I would have to walk *right through* her misty cold presence to get to the first floor.

I gritted my teeth and walked down the steps toward her. I gasped as I reached the curve in the staircase. I felt the watchful spirit's presence surround me, and cold shivers chased up and down my body. My knees started trembling, and I hurried around the bend, almost stumbling in my haste. My friend had already reached the ground floor, and she stared up at me in concern as I wobbled down the final steps, cold as ice and shaking all over.

"Let's get out of here," I muttered and hurried to the back door on shaking legs. My hands quivered so much I could hardly turn the handle, but a moment later I was out on the porch. I went straight to the outer staircase and dropped heavily onto the first step, gasping in the fresh air. My whole body trembled with cold, as if I'd been standing in the snow. My friend sat beside me, and I gave her a brief explanation about the ghost. She nodded, knowing from previous conversations that I was psychic. This was the first time she'd seen it in action, though. We'd never visited a haunted house together, until today.

It took me a good five minutes to get over the shakes. Then I hurried us through the self-guided portion of the tour and over to the visitor center. After a hasty visit to the gift shop, we headed back to the parking lot. I don't think I managed to take a proper deep breath until we were off the grounds and driving back toward town.

Two ghosts in one day were one too many, I decided. The next time we visited the Hermitage, I'd stick to walking the grounds. Maybe I'd find Rachel wandering through her gardens and we could have a nice chat. But I'd skip the house tour. I wasn't messing with the spirit on the stairs again.

7

Fiddling Contest

I was just a young chap back in those days, but I was already a county clerk, and I had ambitions to become a judge. I was at the county court the day the wall of the jailhouse fell out. This was a real tragedy, though I suppose the criminals didn't mind, because the county court didn't have enough money to fix the jail. All the prominent citizens gathered round the scene of the disaster, wondering what to do. Finally, I suggested we get up a fiddling contest. Folks hereabouts would come from miles around to hear a good fiddler play, and we could raise the money in no time flat.

"Great idea, Fred," Coot Kersey said heartily. He was the best fiddle player in the county.

Everyone nodded enthusiastically, and the doctor said, "We'll have to notify Ples Haslock."

This brought cheers from everyone but Coot. In those days, we had fiddlers who could bring tears to the eyes of the most hardened criminal. They could make their fiddles sing, screech, cry, and play the sweetest music this side of the heavenly realms. And the best of the best was Ples Haslock.

FIDDLING CONTEST

Ples Haslock drew a crowd every time he picked up his fiddle. He fiddled for all the local parties and dances, sometimes going fifty miles or more because the folks in these parts figured a party wasn't a party without Ples and his fiddle.

Ples had taught himself to play the fiddle when he was quite young. His daddy had traded an old horse for a bunch of junk being peddled by an Irish gypsy, and Ples found a fiddle box among the crates. Ples made some strings for the old fiddle box, and soon he was playing better than all the other fiddlers in the area.

Just hearing that Ples was going to play drew large crowds to the local fiddling contests, but it got so that it was hard to get any other fiddlers to sign up for a contest. Once they knew Ples was going to fiddle, they knew they had no chance of winning. Ples always walked off with the prize—usually a gallon of fine drinking whiskey—at every fiddling contest in the district. Folks started offering a jug to the second-place winner so other fiddlers would sign up for the contests. The fiddlers all vied with one another over that second jug; they never bothered about the first one. No one ever beat Ples, and well they knew it.

"I hear that Ples is down with heart dropsy," Coot Kersey said to the folks gathered around the collapsed jailhouse wall. "Maybe he can't come this time."

"Or so you hope, eh Coot?" Everyone laughed, even Coot.

"I'm heading over that way on business tomorrow," I said. "I'll stop by and notify Ples of the contest."

"You're a good man, Fred," ol' Doc Smith said.

Everyone decided that the jailhouse benefit fiddling contest would take place two weeks from that Monday, and the crowd dispersed. In the morning I drove over to Ples Haslock's place and stopped my wagon in front of the house. The house—a one-room shack, really—was looking dilapidated. The shingles were beginning to curl up on the roof, and some of the clapboards had dropped right off.

"Ples Haslock," I called out. "You home, Ples?"

No one answered from the house. I climbed the shaky steps to the porch.

"Who's there?" Ples called from inside.

"It's Fred Bennett from Dukedom."

"Come on in," Ples called at once. "I haven't seen you in a coon's age. How's your folks?"

I went into the one-room house, which was filled with clutter—old clothes, pots, pans, and junk of all sorts. Ples was lying in bed at the far end of the room under a heap of old quilts, his fiddle beside him. I was shocked at how pale and ill Ples looked. His face had shrunk and was tinged with green, and there were big liver splotches on his face and hands.

"My folks are doing well," I said. "How are you feeling, Ples?"

"Feelin' a might poorly," Ples said, his long fingers plucking gently at the strings of his fiddle. "I don't reckon I know what I'd do if it weren't for my kind neighbors. The women bring me things to eat three times a day and sit talking with me. The menfolk check up on me at night to make sure I ain't fell out of bed or be ailin' and need help. Between visits, I just lie here and play my fiddle."

"I heard you were ailing," I said, dropping into a chair beside him.

"That's a fact," said Ples. "The heart dropsy runs in the Haslock family. I've been having a bit of a rough time, but I aim to be up and about soon."

"That's good news, Ples," I said, wondering if I should tell him about the fiddle contest. I decided it couldn't hurt anything, so I told him all about the jail wall falling in, making a story of it like he used to tell me stories when I was small. When I got to the part about the fiddle contest, Ples perked up.

"I'll be there for sure!" Ples was pleased as punch. "When that roll is called up yonder in Dukedom, I'll be there for certain!"

I visited with Ples for quite a while then reluctantly took leave of him. He looked so ill that I wasn't sure if I would ever see him again. But I said lightly, "We'll be looking for you at the benefit, Ples."

"Get that Fiddler's Dram ready," said Ples with a tired grin. "I'm aiming to win it!"

The night of the benefit, nearly everyone in Dukedom turned out in their Sunday best. The contest was being held at the schoolhouse, and everyone hurried in to get a good seat. I sat with my girl near the front, since I was one of the sponsors. The room was filled with the typical sort of frolicking that goes with such a big event: old folks gossiping, boys and girls running about, young men talking loudly and showing off for the girls, who sneaked glances at them and giggled.

Judge Huley Dunlap hurried out on the stage and announced that the contest was about to start. Everyone settled down. Into the relative silence, the judge read the names of the seven fiddlers who would compete. Ples Haslock's name was not among them.

Everyone started yelling: "What about Ples? Where's Ples?"

"Well," Judge Dunlap said. "We've been hoping he'd make it here tonight, but he's been feeling poorly and it's a long way. I reckon he couldn't stand up to the trip. If anybody wants their admission fee back, they can get it at the door."

There was quite a bit of grumbling, but everyone stayed in their seats. The seven fiddlers came out on the stage and took their seats. Everyone in the crowd knew that the first five fiddlers didn't stand a chance. They were just run-of-the-mill types who sat around and sawed at the strings. No, with Ples Haslock out of the running, the contest was between Coot Kersey and Old Rob Reddin.

Well, the first five fiddlers played, and no one paid them any special attention. They were as average as could be. Then came Coot's turn. He was a serious fiddler. He got his fiddle set just right before he started playing a rousing rendition of "Leather Britches." He sawed and fiddled and played stunts on the strings until sweat poured off of him. When he finished, the crowd gave him a rousing handclap.

Then Old Rob Reddin came forward. He was the funniest man in town. Not a word could he say without making someone laugh. When Old Rob played the fiddle, it was as much acting as playing. He winked at his wife, who was sitting near the front, and said, "Hold on to your hats, folks! I aim to drive you wild!"

The crowd cheered. Then Old Rob started fiddling "Hell Turned Loose in Georgia." It was quite a performance. Old Rob bent low with the low notes, lifted his eyebrows to the ceiling when the fiddle played high, and every once in a while he'd throw his bow right up into the air and catch it again. As he caught his bow, he'd shout out phrases like "Ladies, where was your husband Saturday night?"

The crowd was shouting and stomping and whistling when Old Rob finished. Old Rob had won hands down.

The entire audience was watching Old Rob caper about, which was why no one saw Ples Haslock until he had already played a few lines of "Poor Wayfaring Stranger." All heads turned to look at the stage as the sweet sounds filled the hall. We were astonished to see Ples, sitting in the fiddler's chair, tapping his foot softly, his head nodding in time to the tune. Ples looked all pale and sickly, but he had made it just in time to play in the contest. The room rustled as everyone settled quietly into their seats. No one wanted to miss a note of the haunting song.

It was nine o'clock when Ples started playing. He played for more than an hour, straight fiddle playing from the heart, with none of the stunts and shouts of Coot and Old Rob. Ples Haslock could make people laugh and weep when he played, but for those of us who heard him play that night, it was more like entering a dream. Ples played "The Two Sisters," "The Elfin Knight," and about a dozen more songs. When he stopped, the crowd came out of its trance, and everyone surged to their feet. They stomped and whooped, hollered, screamed, whistled, and hammered on the desks. It looked like the crowd was going to tear the schoolhouse down, so great was the excitement.

The crowd cheered so loud, no one heard the speech Judge Dunlap made when he handed Ples the first-place jug of whiskey. Old Rob won the second-place jug, but no one noticed. Everyone was watching Ples as he hooked a finger into the handle of the whiskey jug, hoisted it over his shoulder, jerked the corncob out of the mouth, and took a long pull of whiskey—his Fiddler's Dram.

And then Ples, the whiskey jug, and the fiddle all crashed to the floor. There was instant, stunned silence before everyone rushed to the stage. Judge Dunlap made them stand back, shouting, "Get a doctor! I can't feel a heartbeat."

My girl gave a sob and clung to my arm. We all stared at Ples lying on the stage. While Ples was playing, none of us had noticed that his clothes were covered with clay. Ples looked like he had walked through a swamp, and he was pale as death.

The doctor hurried in and knelt to examine Ples.

"How did he get in here?" the doctor asked the judge.

"He walked in," said the judge, puzzled by the question. "He fiddled for a piece and then keeled over dead before our eyes, poor man."

"Keeled over, my sainted granny!" the doctor exclaimed. "This man's been dead for at least forty-eight hours. And from the state of his clothes, I'd say he'd been buried too."

8

The White Phantom

JACKSON

There once was an evil man who married a rich lady for her money and then hired someone to kill her while he was away. When he returned home a rich widower, the evil man discovered that his wife had hidden her mother's jewelry before her death. They were spectacular specimens: a diamond ring, a ruby necklace, and a small but very fine jeweled tiara. The collection amounted to a tidy sum. The widower looked high and low for the jewels, but he could not find where she hid them.

The widower spent many hours searching for the hidden jewelry. It was all he could think about during the day and all he dreamt about at night. His obsession grew so much that he hardly got any sleep. He spent his nights wandering around in the dark, clutching his head and trying to figure out where his dead wife had secreted the family jewels.

One night, while he was walking along the road that fronted his house, probably searching for a hiding place, the widower came to a swampy area where the creek crossed under a bridge. There he saw a big round ball of fire rising out of the bulrushes. It swooshed over the bridge and came to hover in front of him.

THE WHITE PHANTOM

It floated slowly toward the right and then swooped back to him, acting like a dog that wanted him to follow it.

The widower had heard about the will-o'-the-wisp all his life. He knew it was an evil spirit that lured people into the swamp to drown. So he backed away from the ball of fire, ready to run. But the will-o'-the-wisp followed him, circling the widower whichever way he turned, forcing him to walk to the right.

The will-o'-the-wisp chivvied the widower down the bank of the creek and along the water's edge until he came to a place where the water poured over a high rock. When he reached it, the light vanished with a popping sound, leaving the widower in darkness. He stood listening to the water splash, wondering why he'd been brought to this place. Suddenly he realized that he could hear something talking to itself down in the pool under the small waterfall. He held his breath and strained his ears until he could make out the words. It said: "Go to the Great Oak, mister, mister. Box full of jewels is buried there."

The message repeated itself over and over, until the widower was convinced it must be true. He made up his mind to visit the Great Oak and see what he could find.

Now the Great Oak stood in the middle of the graveyard where they had buried his wife. The widower decided he should visit it in the middle of the night so no one would see him digging for the box of jewels. The next night, he brought a shaded lantern and a shovel and started digging among the tombstones at the foot of the Great Oak.

The widower was waist deep inside a hole when he heard a dry laugh above him. The limbs of the oak tree began to sway and moan. He gasped in surprise and dropped his shovel. When he looked up, he saw a white figure swinging from the lowest branch. It looked as if it was preparing to drop down onto his head. With a gasp of terror, he recognized the ghost of his dead wife.

The White Phantom gave another dry laugh that made the widower's skin crawl, and it sang:

> *I buried my jewels. I buried them low.*
> *My grave is so deep, and my tomb is like night.*
> *I watch over on my jewels wherever I go,*
> *And the white shroud around me is my only light.*
> *You've come for my jewels; I see you tonight.*
> *You've come for my jewels, and I've come for you.*
> *My shroud and my grave put an end to your plight,*
> *For as sure as you're born, I will get you too!*

The widower stood as if he'd been turned to stone, for the phantom's song had put a spell on him. The ghost swung down from the branch and flew in circles around her false husband like an angry bird. She swooped up and down, drawing close to peer into his terrified eyes and run her bony fingers through his hair and then whirling away. She screeched and screamed at him, and the widower could not run away or even make a sound.

The wind moaned through the Great Oak overhead. Lightning flashed and thunder rumbled through the sky. The earth began to tremble, and the bodies of the dead rose from the tombstones around the stricken man. Rotting corpses joined hands with dry skeletons, and they danced in a circle around the man standing waist-deep in his treasure hole while the White Phantom screamed and scratched and pawed at her faithless spouse.

The widower's eyes rolled back in terror until only the whites showed. He collapsed suddenly in a heap at the bottom of the hole, trembling and twitching and howling as his mind broke under the pressure. Two skeletons climbed in after him. They picked him up and tossed him to the White Phantom, who clutched him in her arms and sailed up toward the moon.

The widower was never seen again.

But on nights when the moon is bright and the owls are hooting among the trees, the White Phantom still appears under the Great Oak, carrying the bloody head of her husband in her clawed hands. Faithless spouses should beware, for any that linger too long in the vicinity are doomed to share the false husband's fate.

9

Charlie and the Revenuers

PORTLAND

I applied for a place as a deputy marshal with Revenue Inspector Wheat back in the early 1890s, but the inspector didn't have any permanent openings at the time. However, he was mighty curious about a fellow named John Bradley, who was a moonshiner over in Sumner County. Four different officers had investigated the man and his son, Jimmy, and none of them had come back. The last man to vanish was a war hero named Captain Miller, who'd gone to arrest John Bradley for selling liquor without a license. There was a hullaballoo in Washington, DC, when Miller went missing. The revenue inspector asked if I'd be willing to do some off-the-record sleuthing for him—try to get a job with Bradley and report back what I found. I agreed.

I did some investigating and came across a curious rumor. A fellow named Fleming claimed that Bradley's house was haunted. He'd skedaddled to Texas shortly after telling folks his story and had not returned, so I took a train down to Dallas to interview him before applying for a job with Bradley.

The former Portland resident had a very strange story to tell. According to Fleming, his neighbor John Bradley was having problems with his prize-winning horse. Every morning for a

CHARLIE AND THE REVENUERS

week, when Bradley went to the stable to saddle up his horse, he found the gelding so tired and worn out that it couldn't be ridden. Bradley was convinced that someone was sneaking into the stable each night and riding the gelding all over the county. To what end? Bradley wouldn't say, but Fleming believed the culprit was probably a revenuer, looking for evidence of moonshining.

Bradley was determined to put a stop to the mischief, so he bought a big fancy lock and installed it on the stable door with his own two hands, trying to keep the illicit rider away from his horse. But the next morning, the gelding was still as tired and sore as if he'd been ridden all night. Bradley was furious. He swore he'd shoot whoever was pulling such a dirty trick on him.

Bradley asked Fleming—who was a neighbor of his—to get his gun and help him keep watch so they could catch him in the act. They examined the fence all around the lot to make sure it was solid, then they locked up the front gate and Bradley put the key in his pocket. He had Fleming stand watch by the gate while he took a spot round the back of the stable where the horse was kept.

Around midnight, Fleming heard both barrels of a gun go off behind the stable. Then the door of the stable opened and Bradley's horse stepped out. In the saddle was a big fellow wrapped head to toe in a white sheet that flared over the gelding's withers. The rider was glowing with a ghostly light that cast shadows around the horse. He rode slowly toward the main gate, where Fleming kept watch.

Fleming was so scared his shook in his boots, but he held his ground, hoping this was just some kind of joke. But when the white rider vanished a few feet in front of him, Fleming took off running around the stable. He was sure something must have happened to Bradley, but the moonshiner met him halfway around the building and asked him what he'd seen. Fleming told him about the phantom rider who vanished when he reached the gate.

Bradley said: "Flemming, do you believe in spirits?"

"Not until just now," Flemming replied.

The next evening, Flemming was out inspecting a newly fallen tree in his pasture when he saw Bradley and his son, Jimmy, carrying a couple of shovels and a trunk that looked as if it might contain a dead body out of their barn. They crossed the lane and tossed the trunk and shovels over the fence behind the big hickory that stood by the road. Neither man saw Flemming, since he was hidden by the foliage of the fallen tree, and he thought it best to keep still and watch rather than confront them. The men carried the trunk and shovels along a path that led into some dense woods with a big tulip poplar at the center. Fleming lost sight of them when the land sloped downward.

A couple of days later, Jimmy Bradley dropped by and asked Fleming to go night fishing with him. It was nearly midnight when they returned home with their catch. As they drew near the big hickory on the side of the lane, a phantom materialized before them. He was sitting on the roots of the tree, and he beckoned for them to follow him. Fleming recognized the spirit immediately. It was the ghost he'd seen riding the gelding out of the stable on the night he stood guard with John Bradley. Then the ghost rose, walked through the fence, and headed straight down the path toward the big tulip poplar without looking back.

Fleming sold his farm the next day and moved to Texas.

I thanked Fleming for telling me the tale, and I thought long and hard on what he said during the train ride home.

When I approached John Bradley for a job, he liked my credentials so much that he hired me on the spot. I started work right away, and his son, Jimmy, and I struck up a friendship. We'd go fishing together in the evening or play darts or get up a hand of cards with some of the other fellows working for the Bradleys.

About a week after I started my new job, a young fellow called Charlie Moore—who was courting Jimmy's sister—came to invite Mrs. Bradley and her daughter to a quilting bee with his mother and the ladies from church. Afterward, there was going to be a dance, and he asked me and Jimmy to attend. It was a pleasant way to spend the evening, and my eye was caught by a pretty redhead who had a sharp wit and sparkling eyes. We danced a few times and drank some lemonade, while Mrs. Bradley beamed and nodded her approval. As we mingled, I noticed that Charlie Moore seemed nervous whenever Jimmy came around. He'd turn pale, stammer a bit, and edge away. It seemed strange for a young man who had known Jimmy from the cradle.

I made a point of leaving the dance at the same time as Charlie, and I asked him to show me the way back to the Bradleys' place since I was a newcomer to the area. Charlie was happy to do so, and he chatted to me about his courtship and the probability of its success all the way down the road.

We drew near the Bradleys' place, and Charlie's happy conversation ceased abruptly. He gasped and grabbed my arm, pointing toward the big hickory tree that stood by the side of the road. Rising up from his seat on the roots of the tree was the white figure of a man. He wore long flowing robes that lashed back and forth as if blown by a high wind, though none was blowing. The phantom beckoned for us to follow him. Then he stepped around the tree, floated through the wood fence, and headed down the path through the dense woods toward the tall tulip poplar at its center.

Charlie gasped: "Captain Miller!" Then he fainted.

I gazed after the ghost with a frown, watching until it disappeared into the valley. Then I hauled the unconscious lad over my shoulder and carried him to the bunkhouse, explaining to the other workers that Charlie was too drunk to walk home.

My duties kept me busy until shortly before the noon meal. While Jimmy and some of the others took a rest after lunch, I slipped away and went into the dense woods, following the path the ghost of Captain Miller had taken the night before. At the foot of the big tulip poplar at the center, I found signs of digging. An area several feet in diameter had been disturbed. The sod had been cut and then replaced, and leaves had been hastily scattered over it in an unconvincing way. I moved several pieces of the cut sod and dug into the loose dirt with my hands, going down about a foot. When I tested the dug-out area with my pitchfork, the prongs touched something hard a couple of feet down. Bull's-eye. I hastily replaced earth, sod, and leaves and returned to my duties. Jimmy and the other workers joined me a few minutes later.

I reported my findings to Revenue Inspector Wheat and the proper authorities, who secretly dug up the trunk buried under the tulip poplar. They found the body of Miller packed inside. His arms and legs had been removed from his body to make it fit the dimensions of the trunk and were tucked underneath his torso.

I was convinced that Charlie Moore was the key to arresting Bradley. I met several times with the local revenue officers, and we came up with a plan. The next time Charlie came to the Bradleys' place to court his girl, I offered to help him carry several baskets full of baked goods home to his mother.

The path to the Moores' house led across a stream with steep banks. Charlie crossed the stepping stones and cheerfully climbed the path to the top, with me directly behind him. He stopped abruptly, reeling backward and dropping his baskets so they tumbled down toward the stream. I dropped my own baskets and clapped a hand to Charlie's shoulder to keep him from rolling down after them.

In front of us, the clearing was lit by a strange red light that seemed to emanate from the ground. In the center of the clearing was an old hair trunk that gleamed with a phosphorescent light. The top of the trunk was thrown back at a forty-five-degree angle, exposing the face, torso, and limbs of a dead man.

Three figures in death masks and white shrouds rose straight out of the earth before us. They were carrying a scythe, a pitchfork, and a large Bible. The spirit with the scythe lowered the edge until it touched Charlie Moore's side. The one with the pitchfork did the same to me.

Charlie Moore moaned and sank to the ground, as limp as a rag doll. I grabbed him under his arms and hauled him up, hissing, "Get ahold of yourself, man, if you want to make it out of here alive!"

The figure with the Bible waved at the trunk and intoned: "Frail mortals, who is this man?"

I stiffened and replied: "Spirits, I never knew him in life, and I do not recognize him in death."

The spirit turned toward Charlie Moore, who was trembling like an aspen leaf. I clamped my arm around his thin waist to keep him upright. "Come on, Charlie, say something," I hissed. "These spirits are going to kill us!"

Finally, Charlie got enough gumption to speak: "I . . . I don't know him. Not really. I just know John Brad . . . Bradley and his son killed him. And they made me cut him and bury him in the box in the stable. I heard them call him 'Captain Miller,'" he finished with a rush. With a wail of despair, he collapsed against my chest. I reeled back under his dead weight, and we fell to the ground in a tangle of limbs as the lights went out. The spirits—who were revenue officers in disguise—silently dispersed.

When Charlie came to, I told him he had to go to the authorities at once or the spirits would return and claim his soul. We hightailed it away from the clearing and hurried to the sheriff, where Charlie made his confession. The Bradleys—father and son—were duly arrested, and evidence was brought forth showing their guilt. But John Bradley was allowed out on bail due to a series of squabbles within the court. As soon as he was out, John Bradley went at once to the Moores' home with his gun to "square up" with Charlie Moore. Charlie saw him coming and hid himself away. But Mrs. Moore was made of sterner material. When Bradley showed up on her doorstep, she took down her son's double-barreled shotgun and fired both barrels into his chest and face, killing him instantly.

By the time Jimmy Bradley's case was called in court, he had lost his sanity and was subsequently confined to an asylum in middle Tennessee. Mrs. Moore was acquitted of murder, and she returned home.

The last I heard, Charlie Moore had packed up his mama and moved to Texas to start afresh. As for me? I married that pretty redhead and moved to Nashville to work for Revenue Inspector Wheat as a deputy marshal. But I never again encountered a case that was solved for me by a ghost.

Rest in peace, Captain Miller.

Cab Fare

One evening in May of 1906, I sat dozing in the box of my horse-drawn cab, which was parked on the corner of West End Market and Carden Avenue, when I felt someone tap my knee to get my attention. The touch was cold as an icicle. It jerked me right out of my doze, heart pounding with fear. I looked frantically around for the source. Down on the sidewalk, a young man gazed up at me with eyes that shone as bright as stars.

I'd never before seen a man dressed like that. I thought maybe he was an actor from the theater, so strange was his appearance. His tall hat was bigger at the top than at the bottom, and the brim was rolled up on the sides. He had a cravat round his neck instead of a shirt collar. His coat was green with brass buttons that were as big as silver dollars, and it had long tails in the back. His pants were tight and strapped down under his tall boots. He looked very strange, standing there in the moonlight, gazing up at me with his too-shiny eyes under his top hat.

"I want you to drive me up the road," said the man with the shiny eyes. "I'll tell you when to stop."

"Yes, sir," I said, nodding respectfully.

CAB FARE

He was a strange man, sure enough, but a fare was a fare. I waited for him to get in the back, and then I drove up the road he'd indicated, heading out of town and . . . who knows where?

It was a mighty peculiar ride. At first, things seemed normal. The horses walked briskly along the road, passing through the familiar sights and sounds of the city. But when clouds rolled over the full moon, a strange mist arose around the cab. With the mist came darkness and a sudden feeling of immense speed as if time and space were turning backward. I had the strangest feeling that each step taken by my horses covered miles instead of feet. Shivers ran up and down my spine as I drove. All the houses and trees and bushes and fields bordering the road turned into one long, dark blur.

Suddenly, the full moon sailed out from behind the clouds, filling the road with silver light, as bright as day. The mist vanished as suddenly as it had appeared. At the same moment, the passenger banged on the roof of the carriage, calling "Stop!"

It was a strange place to halt. There were open pastures all around the road, with a few clusters of trees here and there. A few cows dozed in the field on our left, but they were the only living things I could see hereabouts. There were no houses, outbuildings, or barns.

I stopped the horses, and he opened the door and stepped out. "Stay here," the young man with the shining eyes commanded. "I will return." He turned and strode off rapidly along a path that led through a field to a stand of trees in the distance.

I admit, curiosity got the better of me. What in the world was this all about? Who in their right mind would hire a cab, drive into the middle of nowhere, and stalk off into the woods? I set the brake, tied off my reins, and slid out of the driver's box. I silently followed the young man with the shining eyes through the field and into the woods.

It was a smallish wood, and the path spilled me out into a clearing. I ducked behind the last tree and peeked out to see the young man with the shining eyes talking to a fellow who'd been waiting for him in the field.

A few yards away stood two more men. One was just a regular-seeming person, but the second caught my eye. He was tall with a grim jaw and hair that stood straight up on the top of his head. He was dressed as fancy as the young man, with a high collar, a long loose coat, and tight pants that strapped down into his boots. His demeanor was one of stern authority. Right there and then, I decided that I did not want to cross a man like that, not for any money. I crept deeper into the shadows, wondering if I should return to the cab to avoid any possible contact with the stern man.

There was a flurry while two men paced off the ground in the clearing. From their words and actions, I deduced that my fare was going to fight a duel with the stern man. The seconds directed the young man with the shining eyes to stand at one side of the marked area, while the tall stern man took his place on the opposite side, his body at an angle. The seconds handed each of the men a pistol. One of the witnesses stood up and dropped a handkerchief. The young man with the shining eyes shot first, and it looked as if he hit the stern man in the chest. But the tall man did not fall. Instead, he took careful aim while the young man with the shining eyes was forced by the rules of dueling to stand still. The stern man's pistol stopped half-cocked, so he drew back the hammer and aimed again. His bullet hit the young man with the shining eyes in the chest.

My fare fell bleeding onto the ground, and the others clustered around him. They picked him up and started walking toward me, and I realized they were going to carry him to my cab. I made tracks, and by the time they arrived at the road, I was sitting up on the box pretending to be asleep.

They put the young man with the shining eyes into the cab and told me to drive him home. I turned the cab as best I could in the narrow lane, whipped up the horses, and headed back the way I'd come. A mist enclosed the cab as I drove, and the feeling of time and distance moving faster than normal crept over me once again. Occasionally, the young man put his head out of the window and told me which way to turn. With each utterance, his face appeared paler, and his eyes began to glow with a red light as if he were a phantom returned to earth instead of a sick young man. By the time we turned in at the gate leading to his house, my fare looked as if he'd been dead for a hundred years.

I'd been driving around this county my whole life, but I had never seen that house before, or any of the surrounding countryside. I had no idea where we were, and I had no idea how I was going to get back to Nashville once I dropped off my fare. I thought I might tumble off the box of the cab from sheer anxiety. My throat was so tight that it felt like the devil was clutching at my windpipe, but I kept going up the driveway to the darkened house, carrying a dead man back to his people.

When I stopped in front of the veranda, the house lights came on all at once. People swarmed out the front door. A young woman began to weep when she saw the dead man lying in my cab. I figured she must be his wife. They carried the body into the house, and a servant told me to park in front of the house in case I was wanted. I'd just as soon have driven away, but since no one had paid my fare, I hunkered down fretfully to wait for my money. I was done with all this strangeness. I wanted to go home.

Clouds rolled over the moon, and the strange mist grew thicker around me until I could no longer see past the sides of my cab. I grew drowsy and finally dozed off in the thick darkness, still waiting for someone to come out of the house and pay my fare. When I awoke, it was dawn, and my cab was once again sitting on the corner of West End Market and Carden Avenue in Nashville.

I was beyond frightened by my ghostly experience, but it made a good story, so I used it to entertain folks who rode in my cab. One fellow listened with interest to my tale and then insisted I drive him over to the Hermitage and take a tour of the house with him. It seemed a might strange, but he was willing to pay for us both, so off we went. During the tour, the fellow showed me an old painting that was hanging on the wall, and I recognized the person in it at once. It was the stern man who had killed my fare.

"Who is that?" I gasped, chills icing my skin.

"That is General Andrew Jackson," the fellow replied. "He is the one who killed the young man whose ghost you saw, back in May of 1806. And—if my recollection is correct—the young man was buried on a plantation that was originally located at the intersection where you picked him up."

One Pair of Hands

MEMPHIS

My daughter, Jenny, was an Elvis fan. She collected all the albums, watched all the movies, read every article in every magazine. She worked after school every day so she could afford concert tickets when the King came to our area and considered that day one of the highlights of her life.

Jenny met a nice boy in college who shared her Elvis obsession. They got married at the Aladdin hotel in Las Vegas, just like Elvis and Priscilla. Their wedding attire was a near duplicate of the famous couple's.

Jenny was devastated when Elvis passed. She was a mother of two little girls by this time, and she fretted over little Lisa Marie losing her papa almost as much as she mourned the loss of her favorite performer.

The day Jenny heard that Graceland would be opened to visitors, she telephoned me at once. She squealed with delight and spoke so fast I had no idea what she was talking about. It took me five minutes to calm her down, at least enough to get a few sensible details out of her. She and Matt wanted to go to Graceland for their wedding anniversary in November. She wanted her father and me to babysit the grandchildren while

One Pair of Hands

they drove to Memphis for an impromptu second Elvis-centric honeymoon. Of course we agreed.

The girls and I spent that fall weekend watching old Elvis films together and drawing pictures of Graceland to give to their parents when they returned.

They never made it home. My darling and her husband were killed in a car accident on their way back from Memphis.

The next several months were a blur of rage and grief and sorting out endless details. We had to plan and hold the funeral, sign papers to confirm legal custody of our granddaughters, sell their house in Franklin, enroll them in an elementary school near our home, arrange for grief counseling for the whole family, and so much more.

I felt numb inside, as if my mind, body, and soul had frozen at the moment of Jenny's death. Our only child was gone too soon, and I couldn't handle the thought. Instead, I made the task of settling her children into their new life a priority over my personal grief.

Our grief counselor was a smart woman. She picked up on my reluctance to grieve and came up with a solution. She suggested that my husband and I take some time away to rest, recover, and mourn after the girls finished the school year. In early June, we sent the girls to Kentucky to spend their summer vacation with Matthew's parents. Then my husband and I drove to Memphis together to retrace our daughter's final days and mourn.

It was much harder than I thought it would be. I held my emotions in check when we packed the car, and I kept up a cheerful chatter on the drive to Memphis. I exclaimed in delight over the fancy hotel my husband had booked for us and choked down the delicious meal we ordered on our first night. It tasted like sawdust, but I don't think it was an issue with the chef.

After dinner, my husband took me out on the town. We strolled down Beale Street and stopped for a drink at a lively bar playing jazz music. The musicians were top-notch, and the crowd was enthusiastic. I was having a good time, the first fun I'd had since Jenny died. It felt as if a tiny corner of my numb heart was melting.

As we settled down to sleep in our comfortable hotel suite, my husband suggested a trip to Graceland in the morning. I did not want to go to Graceland. I did not want to have anything to do with Elvis ever again. I knew it was nonsensical, but I blamed Elvis for Jenny's death. If she hadn't been obsessed with the King, she and Matt wouldn't have gone to Memphis, and they wouldn't have been driving on the highway when the tractor trailer overturned, killing them instantly.

Rodney, bless his heart, had figured this out months ago, when I'd packed everything Elvis away after Jenny's funeral. The King had been a daily presence in our home since Jenny was a little girl. But now our house was an Elvis-free zone.

Rodney once told me he wanted Jenny's children to share their mother's love of Elvis. It was a bond they could cherish through the years, even when Jenny's memory grew dim. But I just couldn't do it. Not then. Not now.

But I'd have to. For Rodney. For the girls. For Jenny and Matt. Tomorrow, I would face the King and everything he stood for, including the death of my only child. I rolled over and pulled the covers over my head, wishing I could cry. But my eyes were dry, my heart was numb, and I was going to Graceland.

Rodney took care of everything the next morning. He drove the car to the ticket office across the street from the mansion, he paid ten dollars for two tickets to Graceland, and then he guided me into the waiting van that would transport us across the street.

It was a cloudy day, quite cool for summer, with rain predicted for the afternoon. The weather kept the crowd small, and I wasn't sure if this was a good or bad thing. A large crowd could be a distraction. But there were only a few of us in the van, and my heart sank as we drove toward those iconic wrought-iron front gates designed and built by Abe Saucer. They were shaped like a book of sheet music, along with green-colored musical notes and two mirrored silhouettes of Elvis playing his guitar.

As we swept along the drive toward the two-story Colonial Revival house with its side-facing gabled roof and two-story portico, my stomach roiled with nerves. I hastily unwrapped a peppermint to keep from vomiting. Rodney rubbed my shoulder comfortingly, and when the van stopped in front of the house, he helped me down and kept his hand under my elbow to steady my trembling legs.

Flanked by two marble lions, four stone steps ascended to the portico and its four Corinthian columns. The sidelights around the doorway contained colorful and elaborate stained glass. Above the main entrance was a rectangular window, complete with a shallow iron balcony.

As I gazed upward, my eye was caught by a man looking out one of the double-hung windows on the second floor. After a moment of uncertainty, I decided he must be an Elvis impersonator, probably one of the tour guides dressed up as the King. He would make some kind of grand entrance during the tour; maybe he'd sing an Elvis song. A chill ran across my shoulders and down my spine at the thought.

"Come inside," Rodney said gently.

I braced myself and let him lead me through the doors and into the front hallway.

There were tour guides assigned to each room, and we were expertly passed from one place to the next while they described the contents of each room and discussed various aspects of Elvis's life.

From the entryway, we went into the living room with its fifteen-foot-long white couch, white chairs, china cabinet, and fireplace with a mirrored wall. Peacock-themed stained glass framed the doorway to the adjoining music room with its baby grand piano and 1950s-style TV. The third room was the bedroom occupied by Elvis's parents and later by his grandmother. The queen-size bed was draped in a dark purple bedspread; the bathroom was pink. For some reason, the poodle wallpaper in the bathroom made me chuckle. Inside, I felt a bit lighter.

To the left of the entrance hall was the dining room with a truly massive crystal chandelier. It featured six plush chairs in golden metal frames set around a marble table, all of which were placed on black marble flooring in the center with carpet around the perimeter. The kitchen was closed to the public since it was still in use by the family, so we were guided downstairs to view the TV room, where Elvis watched three television sets at once, and saw his record collection and wet bar. Painted on the wall was the King's lightning bolt logo and the initials "TCB." I choked when I saw it. Jenny loved to draw that logo on her school notebooks and tell everyone it meant "taking care of business in a flash."

I hurried into the next room, swallowing repeatedly to ease the lump in my throat. I found myself in the billiard room, and I was so startled by its appearance that I forgot my grief. The walls and ceiling were covered with yards of pleated fabric, which matched the couch. I stood with mouth agape as the guide for the room talked about the pool table, where the balls were arranged just the way they were in the musician's final days, and a rip in the green felt showed the place where one of Elvis's friends had failed at an attempted trick shot.

Rodney caught up with me, and we went back upstairs to the Jungle Room, a den featuring an indoor waterfall of cut fieldstone and items imported from the state of Hawaii. The guide in the room described how the Jungle Room was converted into a recording studio, where Elvis recorded the bulk of his final two albums, and pointed out a chair that was a particular favorite of Lisa Marie. There was a teddy bear in the seat of the chair. When I saw it, I remembered Jenny fretting about how much the little girl must have suffered when her daddy died. And that's when I lost it.

I bolted out of the room through the closest doorway, hoping I wouldn't set off any alarms. Tears streamed down my cheeks as I hurried frantically along walkways, skirting buildings, searching for a place where I could hide until I got myself under control.

I found my way to a fence-lined pasture where several horses were grazing. I leaned against the bars, weeping uncontrollably as all the pain I'd felt since Jenny died overwhelmed me. The promised rain began as I cringed on the edge of the pasture, and it felt appropriate, as if the clouds and sky were crying with me. I knew I'd be soaked, but I couldn't bring myself to care.

All at once, the rain stopped beating down on my aching head. I glanced up in surprise and realized someone was holding an umbrella over me. It was the man I'd seen in the upper-story window—the Elvis impersonator who helped with the tours. He looked older than I expected, about the same age as Elvis had been when he passed. But this was a happier, healthier version of the King. He almost seemed to glow.

"What's the trouble, little lady?" he asked. His voice was pure Elvis. He sounded exactly like the films and TV shows. It gave me goose bumps.

I scrubbed at my red-rimmed eyes, trying to wipe away the tears, and accepted the handkerchief he produced from a pocket. Then I told him all about Jenny. How she loved Elvis. How she and Matt married in the Aladdin room. About the album collections and the movies and the TV specials we watched repeatedly, and, well . . . all of it.

I started crying again when I told him about the car accident on their way home from Graceland, and how Jenny's death was so tied in my mind with Elvis that I'd tried to eliminate the King from our lives, as if hiding him away would somehow bring Jenny back. Confessing all this to an Elvis impersonator felt therapeutic somehow. As if I was pouring out my rage and my grief to the King himself.

He was very nice about it. He asked simple questions whenever I paused, expressed sympathy, and said he totally understood why I'd put away all the reminders of Elvis after Jenny passed.

"My husband, Rodney, thinks we should share Elvis's records and movies with Jenny's daughters. He wants them to have something their mother loved to hold onto as they grow up," I concluded. "He's right. I know he is. But I haven't been able to do it. I think that's the reason he brought me here to Graceland. So I could face all this. Face my grief and move on."

"Grief's a terrible thing," Elvis said. "My mama died of a heart attack when I was in the army. I was stationed in Germany, and I barely got home to see her."

His eyes were so sad, I reached out and patted the arm holding the umbrella.

"It broke my heart," he added. "She was always my best girl."

He described the funeral, and how he could barely walk after burying her. As he spoke, I cried some more—for Elvis, for Lisa Marie, for Jenny and Matt, for their girls.

Wiping my eyes on the last dry bit of the handkerchief, I said impulsively: "I take it back. I'm glad Jenny was an Elvis fan. It was wrong to blame him—you—for an accident that could have happened anytime, anywhere. The Lord works in mysterious ways. He was the one who called Jenny and Matt home. And your mama. I know that all of them are safe in his hands."

"That's the gospel truth," Elvis said solemnly. "Just like the song: 'Those hands are so strong, so when life goes wrong, put your faith into one pair of hands.'"

I smiled tremulously. "One pair of hands," I echoed.

From somewhere around the corner, I heard Rodney calling my name.

"You'd better take hold of this," Elvis said gently, handing me the umbrella.

As soon as I grabbed the handle, he vanished. He was just gone. Completely.

For the second time that day, I stood with my mouth agape. Where had he gone? There was no place to go. The fields and grounds were wide open in this spot. Nowhere to run; nowhere to hide.

Shivers started running uncontrollably up and down my body, and I had to lean against the wet fence railing to stay upright.

What happened to Elvis?

Rodney trotted around the corner and hurried over to me. He took one look at my face and swept me into a bear hug. "I'm sorry, honey. This is my fault. It was too soon to come to Graceland."

I was still in shock, but I roused myself sufficiently to reassure my husband that all was well. I told him that we'd come this far, we may as well see it through. So he guided me to the memorial garden, where we paid tribute at the graves of Elvis and his mother. I tucked the soaked handkerchief that he gave me under the flowers placed on his tomb.

"Thank you," I said aloud.

Then Rodney and I made our way to the van that would deliver us to the ticket office and the adjacent gift shop. And, finally, home to our grandchildren.

12

A Very Good Dog

MAURY COUNTY

Juba wasn't much to look at. He wasn't one of those fancy pure-bred dogs, no sir. He had a jaw like a bulldog, the intelligent eyes of a collie, and the agility of a terrier. He was so far from beautiful that most folks thought he'd turned the corner and was approaching it again from the other side.

Juba belonged to Uncle Mose, who was an overseer on a tobacco farm in Maury County in the 1880s. He'd rescued the dog from drowning as a pup, and the two had been inseparable ever since.

"He's no beauty," Uncle Mose was fond of saying, rubbing behind Juba's ears. "But he's mighty knowing. I believe he could teach the school master a thing or two, if he could talk."

Juba's tail beat so fast it looked as if his rear end was going to take off.

Folks would see Uncle Mose and his dog walking through the fields on dewy mornings, making sure all was well with the crops. And in the evenings, Juba would sit with Uncle Mose by the fire, chewing on a bone and snoozing. Best friends, the two of them were. Inseparable.

A Very Good Dog

Juba was a sober-minded dog, and he took his duties seriously, both as a guard dog and as a hunter. Uncle Mose never failed to tree a possum or coon with Juba at his side. The pair of them were legendary.

In the fall of the year, when the wild grapes were heavy and ripe and the haw trees were filled with crimson-and-black berries and pawpaws fell to the ground, Uncle Mose and his friends got up a hunt on the night of the new moon. There were possums aplenty in autumn, feasting on all the fruity goodness around them, but they were apt to snap and bite and do some real damage to a dog interrupting their feast. Uncle Mose said, "You take care of yourself, Juba. Possums are powerful sassy in persimmon time."

Juba just wagged his tail and nudged the old man's hand. He wasn't afraid of any old possum. He'd stand up to a coon or a bear or a panther or anything else that stood in his way.

When the hunters were all present, Uncle Mose led the way into the woods. They threaded the thin pathways, walking through the forest with their dogs hurrying hither and thither through the underbrush. The smell of ripe fruit and deep woods filled the air, and the wind rattled the leaves and branches, raining nuts down on the ground around them.

Then Juba sounded somewhere ahead. It was the deep bass note of his possum bark. The hunters exclaimed excitedly, for Juba never failed. The first possum had been treed. They broke into a run, answering Juba's summons.

"We got you now," one of the men cried in delight.

"No playing dead tricks on us," his friend replied. "That possum is going into my stewpot, sure enough!"

When they reached the tree, the hunters sent a man to fetch down the possum, and they secured it with a cleft stick. Then onward they went.

It was a very successful hunt. In fact, the possums were so plentiful that there wasn't any challenge to it. Uncle Mose, the eldest of the group, tired out before the younger men. "I'm for home," he told them at last, and whistled for Juba. Wishing them luck with the rest of the hunt, Uncle Mose set out on the path homeward, Juba on his heels and a fat old possum hanging over his thin shoulder for tomorrow night's dinner.

Above them, clouds were rapidly obscuring the starlight, and Uncle Mose heard the rumble of thunder on the horizon. "We'd better hurry," he told his dog as the forest grew black as pitch. The trees around them shivered and shook, and lightning flashed far too close for the old man's comfort. The wind started wailing as if all the spirits of Hell were approaching. Uncle Mose could hear trees crashing down around him and he started to run, stumbling in the darkness over unseen roots, his clothes torn by grasping briars and his hat knocked askew by low-hanging branches. There were twisters in that thunderstorm, Uncle Mose reckoned. He could read the signs. He had to find some kind of shelter for himself and Juba.

Just as the rain started, a flash of lightning lit the sky and Uncle Mose saw a little white painted church ahead. It was the neighborhood church that he attended piously every Sunday morning but wouldn't set foot near at night, on account of the ghosts that haunted the surrounding graveyard. There was the tall marble shaft that marked the grave of an evil trader who sold his soul to the devil and was doomed to walk the earth every night, tortured by the screams of the people he'd harmed in life.

There was the tiny grave of an infant who cried each evening at dusk, wanting its mother. And that pitted stone over there marking the tomb of the man who murdered his own brother. Every side of the cemetery had its own ghost story, and Uncle Mose believed them all.

But that night, the thunderstorm was more ferocious than any ghost. Uncle Mose didn't hesitate. He ran forward through the nearly horizontal rainfall and pushed open the front door, Juba at his heels. He groped his way along the narrow aisle until he reached the front. There he knelt at the altar and prayed that the Lord would keep the twisters and the hants away. Juba lay beside him, licking his trembling hand in mute sympathy as Uncle Mose prayed.

Suddenly, a bolt of lightning flashed right outside the church, the instantaneous thunder crack so loud that Uncle Mose leapt to his feet in fear. On his right, a wild white form appeared at the window. It was there for a second, and then it vanished.

"It's a haint," Uncle Mose shouted, falling backward onto the first pew. "It's that evil trader haint. He's come to carry us away!"

His heart was pounding so fast he could hardly catch his breath. Juba trotted up and nuzzled his arm until he calmed down.

"We can't stay here, Juba. The hants are more dangerous than the storm," Uncle Mose said. He tottered to his feet, still feeling weak in the knees, and turned into the narrow aisle leading to the front door. Then he stopped with a shriek of pure fear. A few yards away, a white figure blocked the aisle. It glowed in the darkness of the church and slowly rose up, growing larger and wider until it eclipsed the aisle completely. It raised a spectral arm and pointed its finger at Uncle Mose. The old man gasped and fell to the floor, his body shaking like an aspen.

"Oh, Lawd," he cried in terror. "It's come for me! Oh, Lawd, I never pestered you for anything all these years. But I'm asking you now! Lawd, make it quick." His voice died out in a sob. He bowed his head and closed his eyes, waiting for the ghost to take him.

Suddenly, a deep base note echoed through the church. It pierced through the old man's terror, and he opened his eyes in surprise. Juba was sounding. It was the same deep howl the dog made whenever he treed a possum. Uncle Mose saw Juba stalking down the aisle toward the enormous ghost—ears erect, eyes menacing, and heavy growls low in his throat. The dog snapped at the glowing figure, nipping the phosphorescent white mass until parts of it vanished in a sparkle of tiny lights. Slowly, the ghost retreated upward toward the balcony, away from the menacing canine in the aisle.

In a matter of moments, Juba had cleared a space three feet wide and three feet high in front of Uncle Mose. It was just big enough for a man to crawl underneath without touching the spectral flesh overhead. Juba barked commandingly at his owner. The dog's message was clear: *Hurry up and get before the ghost blocks the aisle again.*

Uncle Mose's confidence in his dog was complete. If Juba said it was safe to go, then it was safe to go. With a cry of relief, he scrambled to his feet and dove through the opening his dog had cleared. A moment later, the two of them—man and dog—crashed out the front door of the church and ran for home through the horizontal rain, twisters be darned. If the haint wanted the church, the haint could have it.

They reached the cabin in record time, despite the raging downpour. Uncle Mose lit the fire so they could dry off, but it took most of the night for him to get over the shivers. He patted his dog's head over and over with trembling hands as Juba lay beside his chair by the fire, replaying the terrifying scene in his mind. "It would have been all up with me if you hadn't treed that ghost, Juba," he told his dog.

In the bright light of the next morning, Uncle Mose learned that a twister had blown right through the little white church where he'd taken shelter from the storm. There was nothing left but a few broken timbers and some knocked-over gravestones.

"Juba saved me from the haint *and* the twister," Uncle Mose said, wide-eyed. "Thank the Lawd." He wiped his eyes and patted his dog on the head until Juba's rear end wagged with delight. "You're a good dog, Juba. A very good dog."

13

I Saw the Light

NASHVILLE

It was Kitty who got us tickets to a midweek gospel concert at the Ryman Auditorium. She thought we should have a girls' getaway, just the three of us. We grew up together—Kitty, Maude, and I. We shared a nursery at church and had been inseparable all through high school. We stayed in touch in college, were bridesmaids at one another's weddings, and our families got together often enough that all the kids thought they were cousins.

Maude's contribution to our trip was tickets for the hop-on, hop-off trolley around downtown Nashville. "We can play tourist," she said during our weekly call. "And since its midweek in the middle of winter, we will avoid the crowds."

I booked us a hotel suite with enough beds and baths to make us comfortable. We'd stay overnight in the city after the concert and treat ourselves to a fancy breakfast before heading back to our homes.

I bade farewell to my patient husband, who would babysit our two kids while I was galivanting all over Nashville. Then I pulled out of my driveway and headed toward downtown. It was a dreary day. Rain slicked the streets as I turned onto the

I Saw the Light

highway, but I didn't care. Free days were hard to come by, and today was all about having fun and listening to gospel music at the Ryman. Hallelujah!

I parked at the hotel and met Kitty and Maude over at Hattie B's for hot chicken. When in Nashville . . .

Maude got in line early, so we didn't have to wait for a table, glory be. We just scooted right in the door and sat down with our menus. I'll be the first to admit that I couldn't handle the heat when it came to chicken. I ordered medium, Maude got hot, and Kitty got "shut the cluck up," which had three exclamations points and a burn notice on the menu. I thought we'd have to resuscitate her after the first bite, but our wise server had some bread ready to kill the heat, so Kitty made it out alive. We ordered ice-cream floats all around to celebrate our girls' getaway, and then headed to the nearest trolley stop to start our tour.

When the trolley stopped at the Ryman Auditorium, Kitty grabbed my arm and said, "Let's take the self-guided tour!"

"But we are going there tonight for the concert," I protested. "Why do we need a tour?"

I was overruled. A moment later, we stepped down on the sidewalk beside the auditorium, in front of the narrow alley that separated the Ryman and Tootsies. I was the last one off the trolley, so my friends didn't see me trip on the uneven pavement and drop my handbag. The contents spilled all over the rain-slicked entrance to the alley, just as a fellow in a white cowboy hat and fancy suit slipped out the back door of the auditorium. I was scurrying around, scooping things up and drying them off, when the cowboy came over and handed me my wallet.

"Don't forget this, ma'am," he said.

My eyes widened. I didn't realize the wallet had fallen out of my handbag. Losing it would have been a logistical nightmare.

"Thank you so much," I said, smiling up into his dark eyes. He had a thin, handsome face with sideburns, and he looked as if he'd dressed up for a revival of a 1950s Grand Ole Opry show. His suit had tassels down the sleeves and sparkles on the shoulders.

"It's no trouble," he said. He tipped his hat, scooped up the guitar he'd laid beside the auditorium, and trotted to the back entrance of Tootsies, our next stop after the self-guided tour.

"Who are you talking to?" asked Kitty. She'd come back to look for me once she and Maude realized I hadn't followed them to the entrance.

I waved my hand toward Tootsies and said, "I dropped my purse, and a nice fellow helped me pick up my things."

"Come on, you two!" Maude said, poking her head into the alley. "We haven't got all day!"

"Actually, we do," Kitty argued.

I shouldered my handbag and followed them around the building to the ticket office.

We took the self-guided tour, which included a movie, the museum, and a walk through the famous auditorium. We had the place mostly to ourselves. The cold weather and the rain kept most folks away. On the ground floor, Kitty urged us up onto the platform so we could pose around the microphone as if we were singing for the Grand Ole Opry while a company photographer took our picture, first with his DSLR and then with our cell phones.

"We should have asked that nice man to pose with us," I remarked. "His costume was perfect."

"What man?" asked Kitty.

"The one who helped me pick up the stuff in my handbag," I reminded her.

"Was he in costume?" asked Maude as we climbed back down the steps.

"He looked as if he'd just stepped off the stage of the Grand Ole Opry, circa 1955," I replied. "A real country heartthrob."

"Hank Williams lives again!" Kitty cried dramatically, clasping her heart.

"Junior or Senior?" asked Maude as we made our way up the aisle.

"Senior, of course," Kitty replied.

I glanced back at the stage, trying to picture the way the auditorium must have looked in 1950s. Just then, the sound system came on, playing a Hank Williams Sr. song: "Hey, good lookin'—what ya got cookin'? How's about cooking somethin' up with me?" I sang along as we exited the building, heading toward the back alley and Tootsie's honky-tonk.

Another Hank Williams song was playing as we showed our IDs to the doorman and entered the ground-floor barroom. "I can't help it if I'm still in love with you," the singer crooned from the stage. I glanced over and recognized the man who'd helped me with my handbag! I beamed and waved at him as Kitty and Maude claimed seats at the bar. He nodded back, still strumming his guitar.

I grabbed a seat beside Maude and tapped her shoulder, wanting to show her the fellow who'd rescued my wallet. But when I looked back at the stage, a new group was setting up. My

Grand Ole Opry star was gone. Maude turned and I asked her for a menu to cover my gaffe. *For a fancy performer, that cowboy sure stayed out of the limelight*, I thought, remembering how he vanished when I tried to point him out to Kitty. Oh, well.

We spent a half hour listening to country music and then hopped back on the trolley. We rolled through the legislative plaza, wandered through the farmers' market, saw the capitol building, took photos of Athena at the Parthenon in Centennial Park, and ended our tour at the Country Music Hall of Fame. Hank Williams Sr. was crooning "Your Cheatin' Heart" over the loudspeakers as we stepped in the door.

"Now that I think on it, I believe that fellow was dressed up as Hank Williams Sr.," I told Maude as we made our way through the exhibits.

"What man?" she asked absently, stopping to read a sign beside one of Elvis Presley's custom Cadillacs.

"The man I told you about. The one who rescued my wallet when I dropped my handbag," I repeated a bit impatiently. You'd think they'd remember the incident. It just happened a couple of hours ago. "The man who was singing when we got to Tootsies."

"That was a cover band," Maude said.

"The man who sang before the cover band," I explained. Maude gave me a blank stare and shook her head.

"There wasn't anyone before the cover band. They were changing sets when we walked in," she said in a too-patient tone, as if I'd hit my head and needed first aid.

I rolled my eyes and walked over to look at Webb Pierce's 1962 Pontiac Bonneville, which had silver dollars inlaid in the upholstery and pistol door handles.

We checked into our hotel just before dinner, got dressed in some fancy concertgoing outfits bought just for this occasion, and treated ourselves to dinner at Bourbon Steak. Then we lined up with the other concertgoers and headed into the Ryman Auditorium for the gospel concert. I thought they'd be previewing songs from tonight's concert, but it was Hank Williams Sr. again, singing "Lovesick Blues" over the speakers as we made our way to our seats.

The lights dimmed, the singers came on stage, and the music swelled. It was glorious. We cheered and we sang; we laughed and we cried.

When the first bars of "I Saw the Light" rang through the room, I saw the cowboy dressed as a 1950s Grand Ole Opry star step onto the stage with his guitar. He took his place with the instrumentalists, playing his heart out on the old acoustic guitar, and he leaned into a microphone to sing with the band when they reached the chorus: "I saw the light, I saw the light. No more darkness, no more night." The audience went crazy, clapping along and singing so loud I thought they'd blow the roof off the building. I grabbed Kitty's arm and pointed toward my friend from the alley. She nodded and smiled, and I realized she had no idea what I was trying to say. I gave up and just enjoyed the music. The audience clapped for five minutes after the song. The Grand Ole Opry star slipped away long before the audience settled enough for the musicians to continue the set.

The three of us were radiant with joy as we made our way through the rainy streets to our hotel. We kept singing bits of songs from the concert. "I've never heard such a glorious version of 'I saw the Light!'" Kitty exclaimed.

"It was amazing," I agreed. "And you finally got to see the fellow who rescued my wallet!"

"Who?" Kitty asked, turning to give me a puzzled frown.

"The man in the white suit and cowboy hat," I explained. "He stood behind the bass player during the song. He was playing the acoustic guitar."

Kitty and Maude exchanged glances, then looked at me in concern.

"There wasn't anyone standing behind the bass player," Maude said.

"He only came on for the one song," I exclaimed. "Surely you saw him."

They shook their heads in denial.

I reviewed the scene in my mind. The man stepped on the stage with his guitar. He stood in front of an old-fashioned microphone like the prop we'd used when we took our tourist photo. He'd sung along with the band when they reached the chorus. And, I suddenly realized, I could see the stage set right through his body!

My knees wobbled, and I grabbed hold of Kitty's arm to keep from falling. "Oh, dear Lord. I think I saw a ghost!"

Maude's face lit with understanding. "You mean the ghost of Hank William Sr.? He's supposed to haunt the Ryman Auditorium."

"And Tootsies. And the alley between them," Kitty said, her voice rising with excitement. "All the places you saw the cowboy. And you said he was dressed like a 1950s star from the Grand Ole Opry."

"That's amazing," Maude cried. "I can't believe we didn't see him, Kitty."

I was shaking all over. First cold, then hot, then cold again. My friends hustled me into the hotel bar and got me a drink.

"We kept hearing Hank Williams's songs all over town," I marveled. "Even our trolley driver played one during the tour."

"And he appeared on stage when they sang the gospel song he wrote," Kitty finished. "I wonder why he didn't show himself to us, Maude."

"Maybe he did," she said thoughtfully. "We haven't checked our photos from the Ryman Auditorium tour."

We hauled out our phones and looked through the pictures we'd taken during the self-guided tour. My second to last photo from the auditorium showed the three of us posed around the microphone on the stage. Only in my photo, there were four of us: me, Maude, Kitty, and Hank Williams Sr. He was standing just behind us, smiling that same broad smile that had welcomed folks each week to the Grand Ole Opry show.

My phone was the only one that captured the phantom clearly. On Maude's and Kitty's phones, the ghost showed as a white ball of light hovering behind us.

We looked at one another, wide-eyed, holding our phones side by side.

"Well, praise the Lord," Kitty said finally, overcoming her shock.

"I saw the light," the three of us chorused in unison.

14

I'll Find You

I'll tell you a story passed down from my granny, who learned it from her granny. It's about a traveler who was passing through Rutherford County on his way to the West country. It was raining cats and dogs, as my granny used to say, and the traveler got so tired of being wet and cold and muddy that he stopped at a roadside tavern and asked the man running the place if he could have a room for the night.

Now, that traveler, he had no idea that the tavern keeper and his brother, who tended the bar, were in the habit of killing strangers who stayed with them and stealing all their money to keep for themselves. The traveler was right pleased when the two men welcomed him into the barroom, fed him a good meal, and offered him the best room in the house for the night.

After he'd eaten his fill and sat with his hosts around the fire swapping stories and telling tall tales, the traveler thanked the tavern keeper, took up his leather pack, and went upstairs to bed. He was snoring peacefully when the tavern keeper snuck into his room with an axe and cut off his head while the brother stole all the traveler's money from the leather pouch.

I'll Find You

The tavern keeper buried the traveler in the woods while his brother hid the stolen money under a loose floorboard near the woodstove. When the brother went upstairs to clean the room for the next victim, he found the traveler's severed head lying under the cot. He picked it up, put it into a sack, and buried it behind the barn.

And that's when their problems started.

Most folks agree that the brothers would have gotten clean away with the murder if they hadn't separated the traveler's corpse from its head. The man didn't have any family in the area, and only the brothers knew he'd stopped at the tavern during the rainstorm. When the traveler went missing, his folks would have assumed he was drowned in a river crossing or attacked by bandits. But those brothers didn't give a single thought to ghosts when they buried the traveler's body separate from his head, and they sure came to regret it.

The first sign that something was wrong was when the tavern keeper heard something scratching in the yard near the barn. He went outside, trying to see the critter that was messing up his yard, but there wasn't anything there. Just the sound: *scratch, scratch, scratch.* It happened four nights in row, and the tavern keeper couldn't explain it.

A few days later, one of the regulars at the tavern came crashing into the barroom, all pale and shaking. He'd just seen a glowing figure wandering on the edge of the woods near the barn and mumbling to itself: "I'll find you. I'll find you. Never you mind. I'll find you!" The ghost repeated the words over and over, bending down to look at the ground, and scratching at the dirt like it wanted to dig something up. The regular gave a yelp of horror when he realized what it was and fled to the tavern to get away from the ghost.

When he finished his tale, the bartender handed him a glass of shine, and the regular drank it down in one long gulp. It took several refills to steady his nerves. The other drinkers discussed the tale at length. No one else had seen the ghost by the woods, but everyone had a story to tell about haunts they had heard about. The storytelling made for a merry evening, but underneath the jokes there was a feeling of uneasiness in the room. The tavern keeper could tell that his customers didn't care for the notion that the land around their favorite drinking hole might be haunted.

"I'm sure it was just mist coming off the river," he said to the men as they settled their bill and headed for home. "He must have had a nip of shine before he arrived and imagined the whole thing."

The tavern keeper closed the bar early that night and took a lantern outside into the yard, looking for a windblown cloth or the footprints of a passing animal that would explain the "ghost" sighting. But the grounds were empty, and everything was still except for the wind, which whirled around him in a funny, cold swirl, poking at his chest and arms like a pair of skeletal hands. He shuddered and went inside.

Folks in the community were all stirred up by the story of the ghost. They would stop by the tavern during the day to have a drink or play cards, but every single customer left before dark. The tavern keeper knew it was on account of the ghost. He wanted to deny the tale, but it skated too close to the truth about the murdered traveler. The brothers decided their best bet was to stay quiet and ride it out. As long as no one else saw the ghost, the story would die down and it would be business as usual.

One evening, the tavern keeper and his brother were cleaning the glasses in the empty barroom to give themselves something to do when they heard people screaming out on the road. Grabbing a lantern, the brothers raced outside to see what was happening. The local preacher and his wife came running into the tavern yard in a panic.

"Preacher, what happened, what's wrong?" asked the tavern keeper.

"We went to see old Sister Walker, who is ailing, and we were walking home when we saw the ghost in the woods by your barn," the preacher's wife gasped. "It was scratching at the ground and mumbling: 'I'll find you. I'll find you.' And then it straightened up and—" She broke off, covering her face with trembling hands.

The preacher put his arm around his wife and said, "And that's when we realized that the ghost had no head! Blood was running down its neck and all over its clothes. When it heard our gasps, the haunt stumbled toward us, so we ran to you for help."

The preacher's wife was sobbing, so the tavernkeeper—remembering just in time that the minister abstained from drink—offered her a glass of water. The couple sat by the tavern fire for almost an hour before they calmed down enough to accept the bartender's offer of a ride home in the wagon.

"We've got to do something about the ghost," the tavern keeper told his brother when he got back. "That was far too close to the truth. Folks might question our customers, but they ain't going to call the preacher a liar."

"How do you get rid of a ghost?" the bartender asked.

"I'll shoot it," the tavern keeper said. "Tomorrow night, once everyone leaves the bar. I'm going to walk along the road, and when the ghost appears, I'll shoot it."

"Does that work?" asked his brother.

"It had better work, or you and I will have to pack up and leave," the tavern keeper said grimly.

The bar was empty the next day. Everyone in the settlement had heard the preacher's tale, and they were too afraid of the haunt to visit the tavern, day or night. At least for now. When someone got thirsty enough, they'd be back, the tavern keeper reassured himself.

Night fell, and the tavern keeper got down his gun and went into the yard to hunt the ghost. He marched up and down the road in front of the tavern, stalking the ghost, but it didn't appear. The tavern keeper kept watch from dusk until dawn, but the ghost didn't show itself. It was aggravating, to say the least.

The next night, both brothers stood guard outside the tavern, waiting for the ghost. The tavern keeper picked a spot next to the woods where he'd buried the traveler's body. The bartender sat under the oak tree by the barn, near the hole where he'd concealed the traveler's head. Around them, the air cooled and the stars came out. One hour passed, and then a second. The bartender was nearly asleep when a strange wind came swirling around his body. It plucked at his hair and poked at his chest and arms, like a pair of skeletal hands. He sat upright, his heart pounding with fear, and saw a glowing figure trudge around the side of the tavern. It stooped and scraped at the ground, mumbling, "I'll find you. I'll find you. Never you mind. I'll find you!"

From the edge of the woods, the tavern keeper gave a ferocious yell: "I've found *you*, ghost! And you'll not live to tell the story." He ran forward, took aim, and put a bullet through the glowing form. The haunt straightened and faced its assailant. The tavern keeper gasped when he saw the bleeding stump of its neck rising above its shirt. Silvery blood flowed down from the wound to stain its garments.

Something laughed from the direction of the barn. The tavern keeper glanced toward the place where his bartender brother kept watch. Up in the branches of the oak tree, a glowing head appeared, eyes ablaze with red fire. In the ghastly red light cast by the haunt, the tavern keeper saw his brother slumped back against the trunk of the tree, a bloody gunshot wound marring his forehead. With a thrill of horror, the tavern keeper realized his bullet had gone clean through the ghost and killed his brother instead.

The glowing head laughed again. It was a demented sound that grew louder and louder, until the tavern keeper clapped his hands over his ears in alarm. The traveler's decaying body responded immediately, stumbling blindly toward the tree where its head lay buried. It grasped the trunk with decaying fingers, trying to climb up to the glowing orb. The head came crashing down through the limbs of the tree to meet it. The head bounced on the ground and rolled toward the tavern keeper, red eyes glowing as bright as the noonday sun.

The tavern keeper screamed and tried to run, but the rolling head bowled him over like a ninepin. He hit the ground hard, his leg bone shattering with a loud snap. Above his helpless form, the corpse scrambled away from the tree, desperately seeking its head. Finally, skeletal fingers closed around the blazing orb.

The corpse stood upright and placed the head atop the bloody stump of its neck. Whole once more, the dead traveler looked down on the man who had murdered him and chuckled.

"I told you I'd find you," he said to the tavern keeper. Then he closed decaying hands around the tavern keeper's neck and snapped it.

When folks discovered the bodies the next morning, they reckoned a passing traveler had killed the tavern keeper and his brother. Which was the absolute truth.

PART TWO

Powers of Darkness and Light

15

The Long Way Home

CARTER COUNTY

I was late getting home from work that evening, and Ma lit into me at once.

"Michael, drive the cows in," she called as soon as I set my satchel down.

We'd been keeping the cows in the far pasture, which was over a mile and a half away, high up on the hill. It was past time to drive them in. We'd been bringing the cows to the barn every night, ever since one of our neighbors seen a panther up on the

THE LONG WAY HOME

ridge while he was coon hunting. We didn't want a panther eating one of our milking cows.

"I'll head up there now, Mama," I called, grabbing an end of bread off the kitchen counter to munch on my way.

It was getting close to dusk by the time I came across a big old pine lying smack in the middle of the trail we used to bring the cows home. There weren't no way I was getting the herd around that monstrosity this close to dark. They'd wander every which way through the woods to avoid it, and I'd spend half the night trying to fetch them to the barn. I'd have to drive the cows across the ridge and down the path through the patch of woods where the old church once stood before it burned to the ground fifty years ago. There was a flat field in the center of the woods where you could still see some of the settlers' gravestones if you knew where to look.

The notion of walking through the flat field at dusk made me feel sick to my stomach, but I couldn't see no way around it. It was either go across the ridge and through the church woods or leave the cows in the upper pasture where the panther could get them. One way, the haints might get me. The other way, Ma would for sure get me. I was more afraid of Ma in a temper than a possible haint, so I trotted to the upper pasture right quick, hoping I could drive the cows through the flat field before I lost the light.

It took a few false starts, but the cows finally figured out that we were taking the long way home. I got them moving across the ridge, and we headed down to the patch of woods with the flat field at the center. We turned a corner overlooking the old cemetery, and the cows started running and snorting and jumping. Some of them took off through the laurel patch

105

with their tails standing straight up. I looked down into the little flat field and saw a glowing white globe about the size of a bedsheet moving up toward me and the cows.

My heart started hammering and my body slicked with sweat. It was a haint! Or was it?

I decided it must be one of my brothers playing a trick on me. We were always fussing about, jumping out at each other from behind trees and covering ourselves with bedsheets and pretending to be haints out in the barn. They must have heard Ma telling me to bring the cows home and knew I'd take the long way home on account of the fallen tree.

"Hey, boys, you get out from under that old bedsheet. You fellows don't scare me," I called down toward the glowing white globe in the field. "Stop messing about or I'll tell Mama you scared the cows."

At the sound of my voice, the white globe started rising up from the flat field. The last few cows took off through the laurel, snapping branches every which way as they ran. I stood my ground, mad as a wet hen at my brothers for playing such a dumb trick on me.

The white globe kept rising up until it was nearly ten feet off the ground. The queasy feeling in my stomach came back. I couldn't figure out how my brothers were playing this trick. I could see the grass of the field underneath the white globe, and I didn't see no rocks there for a boy to stand on. The white globe looked as if it was floating in midair.

The white globe started twisting around on itself like it was one of them tornado clouds that come with the thunderstorms. It turned itself into a monstrous black dog. There was white light shining all around the edges of the haint, as if it was standing in front of the sun, and its eyes glowed deep red, like two coals.

The haint started rising up again, until its body was bigger than a house. Its back foot was planted on one of the old gravestones in the cemetery. I recognized that marker. My brothers and I found it one summer afternoon when we were exploring the old church ruins. It was the grave of a five-year-old boy who died of fever over a hundred years ago. The black dog must be the little boy's guardian, I realized, and it didn't look glad to see me.

The haint kept moving on up, its body growing larger and larger with every step. My legs were a-tremble so bad I couldn't get them to move. The haint's glowing red eyes had me mesmerized.

Just about the time that black dog's head reached the top of the trees, I snapped out of my daze and ran down through the laurel, just like the cows. I was hollering something awful, and my legs were going so fast I couldn't keep my balance. I fell head over heels and rolled all the way down the hill until I was all scraped up by roots and rocks and whatnot. I landed in some bramble bushes and kind of levitated myself out of them, leaving half my shirt behind. I was bruised and bleeding in a dozen places by the time I got home.

And there were the cows, already at the house, looking as frightened to death as myself. "I'm taking my axe up there at sunup," I promised the cows as I let them in the barn. "I'll get that pine tree chopped up right quick so we never have to take the long way home again."

16

The Wampus Cat

KNOXVILLE

The missus and me, we were just settling down to a late-night piece of apple pie when we heard someone running real fast across our barnyard.

"Casper! Casper!" a man was shouting. I recognized the voice of our new neighbor, Jeb Thomas. I swung the door open and he ran inside, looking as if he thought the devil was after him.

"Shut the door!" shouted Jeb. "Shut it quick!"

I shut the door and my missus tried to calm Jeb down a bit. Just then we heard a terrible howling coming from the barnyard. Jeb nearly fainted at the sound, and the dogs started whining by the fire. I could hear the other animals out in the barn squawking and mooing and neighing their distress at the terrible howling sound.

I knew at once what was making that sound. It was the Wampus cat. I took down my Bible and started reading Psalm 23 in a loud voice. I knew the Wampus cat couldn't stand the words of the Bible, no sir.

The Wampus cat let out one more piercing howl, and then I heard it crashing back through the trees, away from the house.

THE WAMPUS CAT

I read a few more Psalms just to be safe, then put the Bible back on the shelf and went to help my missus get Jeb into a chair. She gave him some hot coffee and cut him a slice of apple pie. Once Jeb had some pie in him, he was ready to tell us what happened.

"I was out late hunting with my dogs," Jeb began, eyeing his empty plate wistfully. "I could hear something howling out in the woods nearby but thought it was just wolves, and the dogs didn't seem to mind it. The dogs got way ahead of me. I kept calling them, but they didn't come back.

"I was trying to decide if I should keep looking for the dogs or just go home when I tripped over a root and fell. My rifle went flying somewhere. As I groped around for it, I smelled this awful smell. It smelled like one of my dogs had fallen into a bog after it messed with a skunk. I called the dogs again, expecting to see Rex or Sam come running up from wherever they'd gotten to. But when I looked up, I saw a pair of big yellow eyes glowing down at me, and there were these huge fangs dripping with saliva. The creature looked kind of like a mountain lion, but it was walking upright like a person. Then it howled, and I thought my skin would turn inside out. I got up and ran as fast as I could, that creature chasing me all the way. Sometimes it was so close I could feel its breath on my neck! I figured your house was closer than mine, so that's why I came here."

Jeb mopped his brow with his sleeve. He was sweating again at the memory, and his hands were shaking. The missus cut him another slice of pie and poured some more coffee.

"I never saw anything like it, Casper," Jeb said after consoling himself with a few bites of pie. "What in the world was that thing, and how did you get rid of it? And do you think it got my dogs?"

"That was the Wampus cat," said my missus before I could finish swallowing my coffee. "They say that the Wampus cat used to be a beautiful Indian woman. The men of her tribe were always going on hunting trips, but the women had to stay home. The Indian woman secretly followed her husband one day when he went hunting with the other men. She hid herself behind a rock, clutching the hide of a mountain cat around her, and spied on the men as they sat around their campfires telling sacred stories and doing magic. According to the laws of the tribe, it was absolutely forbidden for women to hear the sacred stories and see the tribe's magic. So when the Indian woman was discovered, the medicine man punished her by binding her into the mountain cat skin she wore and transforming her into the creature you saw—half woman and half mountain cat. She is doomed forever to roam the hills, howling desolately because she wants to return to her normal body. They say she eats farm animals and even some young children."

"Well, now," I said when my missus had finished her story, "that's one version of the tale. But myself, I think the truth lies in another direction."

I took another swallow of coffee. Jeb waved his fork impatiently and said, "Go on, Casper."

"Not so long ago, an old woman moved into a small house way back up in the hills near here. She lived like a hermit and acted real unfriendly when the folks hereabouts tried to be neighborly. She was a strange woman, with wild hair and a crooked nose and a way of looking at you like she was reading your mind. It wasn't long before the folks around here started calling her a witch because of the way the cattle and sheep acted after she came. Sometimes the cattle would fall over for no reason at all and lie like they were dead. Or the sheep would walk around in circles till they fell down. Some animals rammed themselves to death against barn walls. It was like someone had hexed the farms in these parts.

"Then animals started going missing, and people really got stirred up. We began hearing rumors about a strange black cat that could sometimes be seen in the barnyards around the county. Folks said the cat was really the witch. People claimed that the witch, disguised as a cat, would sneak into a farmhouse during the day when the door was open. The witch would hide herself somewhere in the house until the family went to bed at night, and then she would put a spell on the family so no one would wake before morning. Once her spell was completed, the witch would go to the barn and steal whatever animal she fancied. No one had ever caught the witch stealing an animal, but everyone knew that she was the one to blame.

"Finally, the townsfolk decided to lay a trap for the witch. One of the farmers had just gotten a fine new ram, which he had seen the witch looking over real carefully one day when the herd was out grazing. The farmer was sure the witch would try to steal the ram, so they set the trap at his house.

"Sure enough, that night the witch snuck into the house in her cat form and put the whole family under her spell. Then she jumped out the window and went to the barn to get the farmer's new ram. Once she was safely in the barn, the witch began to chant the spell to turn herself back into a human. Before she could finish the spell, several men jumped out and captured her. The witch was halfway through her spell when the trap was sprung, and she didn't have a chance to complete the transformation. She had grown to the size of a woman and was standing upright, but much of her was still a cat, including her large yellow eyes and the fangs. The half-woman, half-cat creature was a terrible sight. Because the witch had been interrupted at a critical juncture, the spell could not be completed or reversed. The witch was trapped in this ghastly form forever.

"The witch howled in terror and struggled to free herself from her captors. She was strong as an ox in her new, misshapen form, and she knocked the men to the barn floor. Then she fled, breaking through the closed barn door in her haste, and disappeared into the hills.

"There was no more hexing of the farm animals after that, but the witch still walks the hills hereabouts, and still stalks farm animals when she can. Folks started calling her the Wampus cat, and they stay indoors on nights when the moon is high and the wind blows strong."

"Nights like tonight," Jeb said thoughtfully, pushing aside his coffee cup. "You never said how you got rid of the Wampus cat."

"Like all witches, the Wampus cat can't stand the sound of Scripture being read," I replied.

"Do you reckon it's safe to go home?" Jeb asked. "My missus will be worrying. And I'd like to see if Rex and Sam made it back."

"I'll drive you home," I said. "We'll take my dogs and the lanterns."

"And your Bible," Jeb said quickly.

"And my Bible," I agreed.

"Well," Jeb said as I got my coat. "I wouldn't have believed in that Wampus cat unless I'd seen it for myself. But I believe in it now!"

Jeb wished my missus goodnight and followed me out into the barnyard, glancing nervously into the nearby woods and clutching my Bible as he walked. Jeb helped hitch my horse up to the wagon, and before we left the barnyard, we lit the lanterns and put the dogs in the back.

As we traveled the short distance to Jeb's place, we could hear the Wampus cat howling in the distance. And closer, we could hear Jeb's dogs howling from his yard. Jeb sagged with relief. When we drove into the yard, Sam and Rex came to greet us. After fussing over his dogs for a bit, Jeb turned to me and said, "Thanks, Casper, for coming to my rescue."

I was just turning the wagon when Jeb opened the front door and called out: "I tell you one thing, Casper. I'm never going hunting at night again!" Then he slammed the door shut, and the dogs and I headed for home.

17

Wait Until Martin Comes

There's a story I heard once about a church elder who was riding home from a visit with several poor folks in his parish when darkness fell. It was about to storm, and the only shelter around was an old, abandoned mansion, reputed to be haunted. The church elder clutched his Bible and said, "The Lord will take care of me."

The preacher arrived at the mansion just as the storm broke. He put his horse in the barn and made his way to the house. The church elder walked across the rotten old porch and tried the front door. It was unlocked. When he ventured through the creaky portal, he found himself in a wide entrance hall liberally strewn with dusty cobwebs. He glanced at his reflection in a large, cracked mirror with an ornate gold frame and straightened his cap. Then he caught a glimpse of another room opening off the entrance hall full of sheet-covered furniture. In the dimness of twilight, the sheets looked like ghosts, and the church elder gave a muffled shriek of alarm before realizing what they were.

The church elder was mighty glad there wasn't anyone there to hear his silly yell. To prove to himself that he wasn't scared of haunts, he walked through the downstairs rooms, looking

WAIT UNTIL MARTIN COMES

in shadowy corners, underneath shrouded furniture, and inside empty bookcases. To his relief, the church elder didn't find a single haunt on the main floor.

The church elder retraced his steps to a large sitting room he had found during his explorations. It stood at the end of a long passageway, and an enormous fireplace filled one entire wall. Coal for a fire had already been laid out, and several comfortable chairs were grouped invitingly around the hearth. The church elder thought it was the perfect place to wait out the storm. It was quite a surprise to find such a pleasant room in an abandoned mansion, but the church elder did not question this happenstance. He just went inside and lit the coal fire. Then he settled down in one of the comfortable chairs and began to read his Bible. The fire smoldered in a heap of glowing coals as the storm howled around the mansion and shook the windows. It was really a terrible night to be outside, the church elder thought. He had made the right choice, stopping here for the evening. Imagine trying to ride home in this rain! The church elder put a few more coals on the fire and sat back with a sigh of contentment.

More than an hour had passed in this pleasant manner when the church elder was roused from his reading by a strange noise. He looked up from his Bible and saw a very large black cat stretching itself in the doorway. The black cat strolled over to the fireplace and sat down among the red-hot coals. The church elder swallowed nervously as the cat picked up a coal in its paw and licked it. Then the cat got up, shook itself, and walked to the foot of the church elder's chair. It fixed its blazing yellow eyes on the church elder, black tail lashing, and said quietly, "Wait until Martin comes."

The church elder gasped. He had never heard of a talking cat before.

The black cat sat down in front of the church elder and watched him without blinking. When nothing else happened, the church elder turned back to his Bible, nervously muttering to himself, "The Lord will take care of me."

A few minutes later, another cat came into the room. It was black as midnight and as large as the biggest dog you've ever seen. It strolled over to the fireplace, lay down among the red-hot coals, and lazily batted them with its enormous paws. Then it walked over to the first cat and said, "Shall we do it now?"

The first cat replied, "Let's wait until Martin comes."

The two black cats sat facing the chair, watching as the church elder read through the Pauline Epistles at top speed. Their blazing yellow eyes seemed never to blink.

A breeze swirled through the sitting room, rustling the black cats' fur and tangling the preacher's hair. The air grew colder and colder, dampening the warmth of the fire and the cheery crackling of the flames. A third black cat, big as a panther, entered the room. It went to the enormous fireplace full of red-hot coals and rolled among them, chewing some and spitting them out. Then it ambled over to the other two black cats that were facing the church elder in his chair.

"What shall we do with him?" it growled to the others.

"We should not do anything until Martin comes," the black cats replied together.

The church elder flipped to Revelation, looking fearfully around the room. Then he snapped shut his Bible and stood up.

"Goodnight, black cats," he said politely. "I'm glad of your company, but when Martin comes, you tell him I couldn't wait!"

18

A Terrible Thing Indeed

CLARKSVILLE

I was paying a lengthy visit with my sister and her family in Clarksville when I made the acquaintance of the Widow Jenkins. She was a wealthy young widow, with flowing dark tresses and blue eyes that in happier times must sparkle but due to the death of her spouse were currently dull and tearful. She had no living family and her marriage had been childless, so there was nothing to distract her from her grief.

As a retired clergyman, I felt it my duty to comfort the afflicted, so I paid a call on the lady and listened with compassion as she described happier times with her late husband and wept anew for his loss. It was heartrending.

Afterward, I spoke with the rector of her church, who nodded solemnly and told me that he too went regularly to pray with her. He recommended that we join forces and take her through a spiritual course in the Psalms to help her cope with her grief.

It happened that my young nephew retired from the navy about this time and returned to his old home in Clarksville. He dropped by my sister's home one evening to tell us that he was bored of retirement and had taken a job at the local bank to fill

A TERRIBLE THING INDEED

his days with meaningful work. When he found out I was on my way to counsel the Widow Jenkins, he volunteered to come along, as they had been friends in their childhood.

The Widow Jenkins perked up a bit at the sight of her childhood friend. That evening, her lamentations for her lost husband were eschewed in favor of Scripture reading and reminiscing on the youthful peccadilloes of our retired naval officer. I was pleased that my spiritual ministrations were finally taking hold.

After a full month of Psalm reading, the Widow Jenkins seemed much recovered in spirits. The rector and I met for tea after midweek service to discuss the success of our spiritual counseling.

"It seems as if our counsel will not be needed for much longer," the rector said happily. "The sparkle is back in the Widow Jenkins's eyes, and her demeanor is much recovered."

I nodded with satisfaction. "Yes, her color has returned, and she speaks of her departed husband with fondness, but not the wild grief I remember when first we met."

We planned to wrap up our counsel sessions by recommending that the Widow Jenkins take on a worthy task as a distraction from her grief. Perhaps she could teach the children's Sunday school class when their teacher retired next month. Alas, when I went for my weekly visit to put forth this proposal, I found the Widow Jenkins reverted to a state of extreme lamentation and grief. I was horror-struck. What had happened to overset the widow and set her back to the condition in which I first found her?

It took much persuasion on my part to get her to reveal her tale. According to the good lady, her departed husband had appeared to her in a dream and demanded that she open the vault where he lay and pay her respects to him one more time. I was horrified by this notion, and the lady was overcome with tears at the thought.

"It is a terrible thing," she wailed. "A terrible thing indeed!"

I counseled the Widow Jenkins to ignore the dream, and then read her a comforting Psalm without once mentioning the children's Sunday school. It was obviously too soon for that.

When I returned to my sister's house, I found my nephew playing ball with some young cousins in the yard. He left the children to their devices and came to inquire about my sad demeanor. I told him about the Widow Jenkins's strange dream, and he was very struck by it.

"One should not ignore the requests of the dead," he said heavily. "A ghost is nothing to be trifled with, uncle. We paid attention to divine signs and portents when I was in the navy."

I reviewed my nephew's words many times that evening and throughout the next day. Indeed, the notion weighed so heavily upon me that I went to see the Widow Jenkins two days later, even though our next spiritual counseling session was not scheduled until the following Wednesday. I found the widow in a similar state of agitation, for the ghost had appeared to her two more times and peremptorily ordered her to enter the vault where his body lay to rest and pay her respects to him one more time.

"It is a terrible thing," she wailed. "A terrible thing indeed. I do not want to dishonor the dead! But my husband's ghost will give me no peace on this matter! Whatever shall I do?"

I calmed her as best I could and promised to speak with the rector of her church on the matter. When I described the strange situation, he was perturbed and went immediately to see the Widow Jenkins. He returned to the church within the hour, pale-faced and upset, and found me on my knees before the altar, seeking divine guidance for this thorny dilemma.

The rector knelt beside me and said, "She does not want to dishonor the dead, yet it is the dead himself who begs her to disturb his grave."

I nodded silently. It was a perfect summary of a dreadful situation. "I fear for her health if we do not acquiesce to this request," I said heavily. "Her demeanor is even worse now than it was when I first made her acquaintance. She may harm herself if she does not lay her husband's ghost to rest."

The rector bowed his head in prayer for several moments. Then he raised glassy eyes to mine and agreed.

We asked my nephew to accompany us, since he was at the peak of his health and strength and we were two old clergymen who did not have the strength between us to remove the lid of the coffin. The widow was shrouded from head to toe in black, with a veil obscuring her red-rimmed eyes. We entered the cold, musty vault with the same solemnity as displayed for any funeral procession. The crypt smelled of sadness and death to me, and I would not have willingly entered it for any purpose less dire. Together my nephew and I removed the heavy lid of the coffin.

Mister Jenkins lay stiff and cold in death. His face was waxen but not yet decayed to the point of unrecognition. Weeping softly, the widow stepped forward, swept aside her veil, and bent to kiss her dead husband on his pale cold lips. I confess, my stomach turned at the sight, and I had to clap a hand over my mouth to keep my breakfast in place.

The widow stood meditating over her husband's body for several moments and then whispered: "I have kept my promise to you, Thomas. Now I am free."

I wondered if she was speaking to her husband's corpse or to his ghost. But I did not inquire.

My nephew and I wrestled the lid of the coffin back into place while the rector prayed with the widow. Then he spoke a blessing and we departed from the tomb. The maid met us at the door to the house and tenderly led the widow inside to grieve in solitude. My nephew doffed his hat and stood gazing up at the house long after the door had closed.

"That took courage," he told me, an admiring note in his voice.

"She is a good woman," I said. "Her grasp of Scripture is sound, and I believe her heart is in the right place. Perhaps this second encounter with death will help her turn the corner and embrace life instead."

"I think it will," my nephew said. "Thank you, Uncle Paul, for helping her."

I waited for two days before calling once again upon the Widow Jenkins. In my experience, two days was enough time to rest and recover from a disturbing experience, but not enough time to fall into a depression caused by it. I would read to her from the Psalms and recommend that she begin teaching the children's Sunday school class as the first step toward reclaiming her health.

When I arrived, Widow Jenkins's maid showed me into a private parlor and informed me that her mistress had gone away on her honeymoon and would not return for a month. I stared at the young woman in astonishment, and then anger swept through me.

"What sort of joke are you playing?" I demanded. "Widow Jenkins adored her late husband so much that when his ghost demanded a sign of her conjugal fidelity, she went to his vault and kissed his corpse on the lips! It is not possible for such a faithful woman to have married again so soon. Go fetch your mistress and cease from these pranks forthwith."

The maid smiled and shook her head. "I am not joking, good sir. My mistress made a deathbed promise to her husband that she would not marry again until they met once more face-to-face. She is a woman of her word, and so she refused the hand of her childhood sweetheart when he proposed last week. It wasn't until you brought her face-to-face with her dead spouse one last time that my mistress was free to wed again."

My jaw dropped open in shock. In my mind, everything clicked into place. I remembered the way Widow Jenkins perked up when my nephew returned to Clarksville and the depth of despair she displayed when talking about her husband's "ghostly" demand. The words she spoke over his tomb made complete sense to me now, as did the thanks my nephew gave me on the sidewalk in front of her house.

"That rascal," I muttered angrily. "My nephew manipulated me like a fish on a hook!"

The maid rubbed her mouth with her hand to hide a smile. "I like to think he freed my lady from a promise she should never had made," the young woman said. "They are very happy, Reverend. I think you will be too once you have time to think on it."

"They had best consider it my wedding gift to them," I said gruffly. "For they will not receive another!"

The maid laughed outright. "I will tell them so when I join my lady tomorrow. She left me behind to break the news to you!"

"And left it up to me to tell the rector?" I guessed darkly.

"I believe so, good Reverend," she said, and handed me my hat.

"I get to christen their first child," I told her as she saw me out. "They owe me that much!"

"You will have to sort that out with the rector," the maid said as she shut the front door.

I sighed, clapped my hat upon my head, and went to break the news to the rector.

The Hitchhiker

When I was a young man, I worked as a carpenter, and I made a pretty penny doing it. I married early and already had a couple of young'uns when I was asked to do a piece of work in Chattanooga, building up a fancy house for a rich feller and his wife who took a notion to move there. It was too far to go home each night, so I stayed in an old cabin they had on the property and drove home on the weekends to see my family.

Now I'd bought a secondhand Model T Ford, the very first car owned by anyone in the family, and I was right proud of it. I kept it polished up good and was careful to keep it away from overhanging trees and bushes that might scratch up my paint. I was as protective of that car as a broody hen with her chicks, so I drove her slow and careful up the twists and turns of the mountain and then back down the other side whenever I went home on the weekend, careful to avoid any potholes. I didn't want a blown-out tire up there on the mountain. There was a twenty-mile stretch with no houses on it, and I didn't fancy walking out that far and back for a part if I broke my car on a bump.

THE HITCHHIKER

Late one afternoon when the new house was more than halfway done, I got called to the company phone. It was my wife, looking for me to come home quick cause our young'uns were sick and she needed my help. It was already quittin' time, and twilight was closing fast in the shadow of the mountains. I had a long drive ahead of me up that narrow, twisty road. I'd never driven it at night, so I felt real nervous. But "sooner started, sooner done," as my granny always said, so I gassed up my Model T and headed for home.

A soft summer breeze caressed my face as I drove up the mountain. The only sound was the whirl of my tires, and the only things visible in my headlights were the laurel bushes on the side of the road and the canopy of trees above my head.

I had just reached the twenty-mile empty stretch when a strange, rotten smell drifted through the air. I wrinkled my nose as I rounded the bend and hit the brakes in alarm. Standing in a water ditch on the side of the road was a huge barrel-shaped figure with a hairy body, extremely long arms, and a flat brown face. Its eyes were round and dark, its ears were small, and its nose was flat. Its feet were huge, and I reckoned the man . . . person . . . critter . . . weighed several hundred pounds. I'd never seen anything like it, but I'd heard tell of an ape-critter called a Boojum or a Bigfoot, and I reckoned I was looking straight at one right now.

The Boojum squinted at me in the headlights, as if he was trying to figure out what kind of critter I was. It would have been funny, only my heart was pitty-patting so hard I couldn't laugh right then. After a minute of staring, that big hairy critter stalked up to me, leaned over the car, and stepped on the running board. My mouth dropped open, which was a mistake because, woo-ee, did that Boojum smell—like stale sweat mixed with rotting garbage. I don't know the last time that hairy ape-man took a bath, but he was long overdue.

The Boojum reached down with his hairy arms, which were twice as wide as mine, and opened the door with fingers that were a good ten inches long. He got into the passenger seat of my Model T, as cool as you please. He looked me over, and his big dark eyes had twin flames in them, reflecting the headlight. There wasn't anything I could do. If'n he wanted to, he could scoop me up one-handed and toss me down the mountain; he was that big.

"So, mister, do you need a ride?" I asked in the polite tone my mama drilled into me as a young'un. The Boojum didn't say nothing, just looked pointedly ahead, so I put my car back in gear and started driving carefully down that twisty dark road, avoiding the potholes and washboard sections whenever I could. I wasn't going to hurt my Model T for no one, not even a hairy Boojum hitchhiker that could have ate me for lunch and still had room for dessert.

I was so nervous, my hands were trembling on the steering wheel. But that old Boojum didn't say nothing to me. He just kept breathing heavily, each puff of air adding to the stench in the car. My nose just about stopped working with him so close. It was a good thing I had the windows down, or I might have suffocated.

To break the awkward silence, I told the Boojum about my wife's phone call and my sick young'uns. I had two little ones already and a third on the way. Then I rambled on about my carpenter job down in Chattanooga and about how much it cost to keep up the Model T, and the little apple seedling my wife was nurturing that came from my granny's prizewinning tree. Anything I could think of to pass the time.

We'd gone a good ten miles, and I started wondering if the Boojum intended to come all the way home with me. I was trying to figure out how to explain my companion to Molly when the Boojum shifted suddenly in this seat, opened the car door, and stepped onto the running board. I obligingly stopped the Model T so he could get down, and watched as the Boojum walked over to a barely discernable footpath on the side of the road.

"Have a good evening, sir," I called to him, and stepped on the gas. Getting out of there seemed like a good idea right about then.

I glanced back when I came to the next bend. In the bit of moonlight that filtered through the tree branches overhead, I could see the tall hairy figure standing by the side of the road, watching me drive away. He looked a bit lonesome, to tell the truth. I wondered where he was going, and why it was so urgent that he'd hitched a ride in my Model T. With hairy legs that long, he probably could have gotten to his destination just as quickly walking as he did by riding in my car.

I rounded the bend and took a deep breath in relief. Which was a mistake, cause the car still smelled to high heaven of sweat and old garbage and, well . . . of Boojum. I was shaking and sweating and babbling to myself the whole way home, overreacting to the strange situation. What a crazy adventure. No one would ever believe me. Folks thought the Boojum was just a story people told to entertain the young'uns.

Molly came waddling out to the car to greet me, relief all over her pretty face. As soon as she caught a whiff of the

Boojum's scent, she reeled back and made a run for the bathroom. Carrying a young'un made her sick to her stomach, and that Boojum smell was enough to make anyone lose their dinner.

I followed my wife into the house and went to the bedroom to check on the kids. They were asleep, but they stirred restlessly when they smelled their Boojum-scented papa come in. I beat a hasty retreat before they woke and had me a good washup before returning to the sickroom so Molly could get some rest.

"What in heaven's name was that smell?" she groaned as she curled up on our bed.

"I'll tell you all about it in the morning," I said, tucking her in with a scented sachet her granny had given us to help with stomach ailments.

It took a couple of days to get the young'uns back on their feet so Molly was able to cope on her own. With things back to normal, I finally got a chance to wash the Model T to get rid of the Boojum scent. And don't you know, there were scratches all over the door handle where the Boojum's long fingernails had gripped it! I showed them to Molly when I told her about my adventure.

"I don't mind picking up a needy hitchhiker," I exclaimed. "But darn it, that Boojum messed with my paint job! And just when I'd gotten the Model T polished up good. I'm going to charge him the next time he comes around wanting a ride!"

Molly gave me a funny pursed-lip look that meant she was trying not to smile. "You do that, sweetheart," she said. "You charge that Boojum a dollar for every scratch. That will learn him!"

20

Tailypo

MONTGOMERY COUNTY

Way back in the woods of Tennessee lived an old man and his three dogs—Uno, Ino, and Cumptico-Calico. They lived in a small cabin with only one room. This room was their parlor and their bedroom and their kitchen and their sitting room. It had one giant fireplace, where the old man cooked supper for himself and his dogs every night.

One night, while the dogs were snoozing by the fire and the old man was washing up after his supper, a very curious creature crept through a crack between the logs of the cabin. The old man stopped washing his plate and stared at the creature. It had a rather round body and the longest tail you ever did see.

As soon as the old man saw that varmint invading his cozy cabin, he grabbed his hatchet. Thwack! He cut off its tail. The creature gave a startled squeak and raced back through the crack in the logs. Beside the fire, the dogs grumbled a bit and rolled over, ignoring the whole thing.

The old man picked up the very long tail. There was some good meat on that tail, so he roasted it over the fire. Cumptico-Calico woke up when she smelled the tail cooking and begged for a bite, but after the old man had his first taste,

TAILYPO

he couldn't bear to part with a single mouthful. Cumptico-Calico grumbled and lay back down to sleep.

The old man was tired, so he finished washing up and went to bed. He hadn't been sleeping too long when a thumping noise awoke him. It sounded like an animal was climbing up the side of his cabin. He heard a scratch, scratch, scratching noise, like the claws of a cat. And then a voice rang out: "Tailypo, Tailypo; all I want's my Tailypo."

The old man sat bolt upright in bed. He called to the dogs, "Hut! Hut! Hut!" like he did when they were out hunting. Uno and Ino jumped up immediately and began barking like mad. Cumptico-Calico got up slowly and stretched. She was still mad at the old man for not giving her a bite of the tail. The old man sent the dogs outside. He heard them trying to climb the cabin walls after the creature. It gave a squeal, and he heard a thump as it jumped to the ground and raced away, the dogs chasing it around the back of the cabin and deep into the woods.

Much later, he heard the dogs return and lay down under the lean-to attached to the cabin. The old man relaxed then and went back to sleep. Along about midnight, the old man woke with his heart pounding madly. He could hear something scratch, scratch, scratching right above his cabin door. "Tailypo, Tailypo; all I want's my Tailypo," the voice was chanting rhythmically against the steady scratch, scratch, scratch at the top of the door.

The old man jumped up, yelling "Hut! Hut! Hut!" to his dogs. They started barking wildly, and he heard them race around the corner of the house from the lean-to. He saw them catch up with a shadowy something at the gate in front of the cabin. The dogs almost tore the fence down trying to get at it. Finally, Cumptico-Calico leapt onto a stump and over the fence, Uno and Ino on her heels, and he heard them chasing the creature way down into the big swamp.

The old man sat up for a while, listening for the dogs to return. About three in the morning, he finally fell asleep again. Toward daybreak, but while it was still dark, the old man was wakened again by the sound of a voice coming from the direction of the swamp. "You know, I know; all I want's my Tailypo." The old man broke out in a cold sweat and yelled "Hut! Hut! Hut!" for his dogs. But the dogs didn't answer, and the old man feared that the creature had lured them down into the big swamp to kill them. He got out of bed and barricaded the door. Then he hid under the covers and tried to sleep. When it was light, he was going to take his hatchet and his gun and go find his dogs.

Just before morning, the old man was wakened from a fitful doze by a thumping sound right in the cabin. Something was climbing the covers at the foot of his bed. He peered over the covers and saw two pointed ears at the end of the bed. He could hear a scratch, scratch, scratching sound as the creature climbed up the bed, and in a moment he was looking into two big, round, fiery eyes. The old man wanted to shout for the dogs, but he couldn't make his voice work. He just shivered as the creature crept up the bed toward him. It was large and heavy. He could feel its sharp claws pricking him as it walked up his body. When it reached his face, it bent toward him and said in a low voice, "Tailypo, Tailypo; all I want's my Tailypo."

All at once the old man found his voice and yelled, "I ain't got your Tailypo!" And the creature said, "Yes, you do!" And it grabbed the old man in its claws and tore him to pieces.

The next day, a trapper came across the old man's dogs wandering aimlessly on the other side of the swamp. When the trapper brought the dogs back to the log cabin, he found the old man dead. All that remained were a few scraps of clothing and some grisly bones. As the trapper buried the old man, he heard a faint chuckling sound coming from the swamp, and a voice said, "Now I got my Tailypo." When they heard the voice, the dogs turned tail and ran for their lives.

There's nothing left of that old cabin now except the stone chimney. Folks who live nearby don't like to go there at night, because when the moon is shining brightly and the wind blows across the swamp, sometimes you can still hear a voice saying, "Tailypo."

21

One Fine Funeral

I've been living next door to the Henslee family for nigh on forever, and it saddened me when they died off over the years until only Addie Bell and her brother, Cass, were left at the old homestead.

Addie Bell could have married any number of fellows who courted her over the years, but instead she devoted herself to her younger brother, Cass, who hadn't as much gumption as Addie Bell and just scraped by doing the minimum to keep body and soul together. It was Addie Bell who did the cooking and the cleaning and the sewing. She kept a farm garden, so they had plenty to eat, and she managed all the money for the household, including paying the insurance premiums so they'd have money for their burying when the time came for them to depart this troubled world. As for Cass, well, he'd take a part-time job here and there, never for long. When it got hard, he quit. He was happy to let Addie Bell support the family.

This state of affairs went on for many years, until Addie Bell was well past the marrying stage and Cass was a fine-looking man in his forties. Then one day, Cass came over to sit with me on the front porch and deliver some surprising news. He'd

One Fine Funeral

been walking out with a girl called Josephine Foxhall for about a month, and no one thought much of it. Cass had been courting this girl and that one ever since he was grown, and nothing came of it. So when Cass told me that he and Josephine had decided to get married, you could have knocked me off my porch with a feather, I was that surprised.

"Truly?" I asked.

"Truly," he replied, beaming with pride. "We are getting married tomorrow week."

I congratulated him, as was proper. Then a thought struck me. How would this impact Addie Bell, who had devoted her whole life to her younger brother? I asked cautiously, "What does Addie Bell have to say about it?"

Cass shrugged. "Dunno. I ain't told her yet." Then he grinned and jumped to his feet. "Now's as good a time as any! Wish me luck." He winked at me and loped next door to the Henslee house to speak to his sister.

"Good luck," I said faintly. I had a sinking feeling in the pit of my stomach. I didn't think Addie Bell would be pleased with this turn of events.

I went inside to pour myself a cold glass of lemonade, and by the time I got back to the front porch, the whole neighborhood could hear what Addie Bell thought about the upcoming marriage. She ranted about her brother's laziness, his lack of sense, and how stuck-up she thought Josephine was.

"You're so lazy, you don't even pay your own funeral insurance premiums," Addie Bell shouted. "If I didn't make them quarterly payments, you'd have nowhere to be buried, you rascal. If you can't even do something that simple, how are you going to support a wife? You ain't bringing her here!"

"Josephine's got enough gumption to support the both of us," Cass retorted. "And while we're speaking of the funeral insurance, let me tell you: A man's wife is duty bound to get his insurance. Everybody knows that. I told Josephine you wouldn't mind making her the beneficiary from now on, seeing she's going to be my wife."

Addie Bell hit the roof when she heard this request. I thought she'd been loud before, but the way she started screaming and ranting sent Cass running for the door. "You told her I wouldn't mind?" she roared after him as he bolted down the front walkway. "I'll see you toasting rabbits on a pitchfork in Hell before I let that stuck-up woman collect any insurance that I paid benefits on!"

Everybody on the block was looking out their windows or watching from the porch as Cass raced down the street and skidded around the corner on his way to Josephine's place.

Cass didn't dare set foot in the old Henslee house that night. He slept on the floor at my place instead. He snuck home around noontime to test the waters, and Addie Bell sent him away in a hot minute, screaming awful things about him and his chosen lady.

Cass laid low for another couple of nights before trying again. This time, Addie Bell let him in the house, though she grumbled and complained anytime he tried to mention his upcoming wedding, which was this coming Saturday at the church. Still, she was much calmer than before, so Cass broached the subject of the insurance again, seeing that the agent was stopping by to collect the premium the following day.

"Well, I been thinking about it, and I suppose there's something to what you say," Addie Bell said grudgingly. "I'll make over the insurance as soon as you and Josie get hitched this weekend. But you'll have to pay the company from now on. I'm done with that."

Cass was delighted. He'd promised Josephine that he'd bring Addie Bell around to their way of thinking, and he had! He gave his sister a sloppy kiss on the cheek and ran off to tell his intended bride the good news.

Cass wasn't there when the insurance man came, so he didn't know that Addie Bell doubled the insurance coverage on her brother, so it cost fifty cents a week when before it only cost twenty-five. I heard the two of them bargaining through the kitchen window, which was open to let in the breeze, and I told myself this must be Addie Bell's way of getting even with Cass for marrying Josephine. I didn't think they'd be pleased about the new price, but it wasn't my business to interfere. At least Addie Bell had come around to the marriage, which was a better situation than before.

On Friday night, Addie Bell fixed Cass a fine supper in celebration of their last night together as a family. She made all his favorite dishes: turnip greens, a whole hog jowl, poke salad, corn pone, buttermilk, fried chicken, and a big pot of black-eyed peas with hot pepper chowchow. The smell of that meal wafted over to my porch and made my mouth water. I almost invited myself to dinner, but I figured they'd want to be alone when they said goodbye. After the wedding tomorrow, Cass would live across town at Josephine's place, and Addie Bell would stay by herself in the old Henslee homestead.

I was reading the newspaper on my porch swing when Cass waddled out his front door and sat down on the stoop, looking as happy and satisfied as any man alive after that massive meal.

He waved to me before taking out his old corncob pipe and having a smoke. He was too full to talk, so we happily ignored each other. Cass would be over when he was good and ready to discuss his new life with Josephine, just like he had every night since he got engaged.

All at once, Cass gave a terrible holler and clutched his belly. He bent double and rolled down to the ground, curled up in a ball of pain. As I leapt up in alarm, he shouted: "Oh, help me, Addie Bell. I'm dying! Call me a doctor, quick."

Addie Bell yelled out the window: "Oh hush, Cass. You've eaten too much, that's all. You need some peppermint tea, not a doctor. I'll put the kettle on."

I wasn't so sure. Cass was real pale and writhing on the ground. I ran down my front steps and jumped the fence between our yards. The neighbors across the way came running too, alarmed by the screams and moans coming from the front stoop of the Henslee house.

"Addie Bell," I shouted as Cass made one final spasm and then lay very still. I reached him at the same time as the neighbor from across the street. We bent over him and realized at once that Cass was gone. "Addie Bell," I shouted again. She came out of the house, looking puzzled.

"What's going on?" she asked. Then she caught sight of Cass, lying so still on the ground, and she clapped a hand over her mouth, her eyes going wide.

"It's too late for the doctor," the neighbor from across the street told Addie Bell before his wife could hush him. Addie Bell's eyes rolled back in her head, and she fainted right there in the doorway.

Everyone on the block gathered round poor dead Cass, and they whispered to one another: "Poor Cass! He died hard; yes, he did. He's gone and left poor Addie and poor Josie."

One ancient fellow shook his head and said, "It looks bad for poor Addie, don't you know. When they die hard, they come back to haunt you. Just you watch."

The others hushed him and helped carry Cass into the house. They laid his body out on the bed and put coins on his eyes. Then they turned the mirror and pictures to the wall and started to moan and wail and pray over the departed.

We put smelling salts under Addie's nose till she woke up. I got her a cup of lemonade, but she set it aside and told me she had to call the insurance company right away. I didn't think it was right, calling the insurance company before anyone had even notified the bride-to-be that the wedding was off, but that's the way Addie Bell did things. She got the insurance doctor to come by right away, and he asked her a few questions about how old Cass was and how he died. Then he filled out some papers to say that Cass died of acute indigestion—which means a god-awful bellyache—and that was that, as far as the law and the insurance company were concerned. It wasn't till after Addie Bell called the undertaker and told him to go all out with the funeral that someone finally went over to tell Josephine that the wedding was off.

Once the arrangements were made and Cass was laid out on the cooling board, Addie Bell called some mourners to come in and sit up with her, and that's when she finally started to moan and carry on. It was mighty peculiar. It felt like Addie Bell had done everything backward.

What exactly was going on at the Henslee house, I wondered. How come Cass had died on this particular Friday, the day *before* his wedding and two days *after* Addie Bell bumped up his insurance coverage? No matter which way I looked at it, things didn't seem right. But what could I do? The doctor had signed papers saying Cass died of indigestion, so that was that as far as the law was concerned.

When Josephine looked in, Addie Bell treated her like a long-lost sister, and they cried on each other's necks. It kind of turned my stomach, after hearing the way Addie Bell had raged about the girl just a few days before. I made up an excuse and went home, real disturbed in my thinking.

Folks sat up with the dead for three nights and two days, as was the custom in those days, moaning and mourning with the last of the Henslee family. Then everyone came from far and wide to attend Cass's funeral. The church was packed full, until the walls almost bulged out. Old, young, rich, poor, near, and far—everyone came to the church to send Cass Henslee off in style.

Addie Bell had gone all out for the funeral, what with all the extra money she'd gotten from the updated insurance policy. There was a fancy awning stretched over the six-by-six hole at the grave site so folks attending the ceremony would stay dry in case of rain. There was a striped canopy running from the church door all the way out to the street. They'd decorated the old church from floor to rooftop with ferns and flowers and black ribbons. Addie Bell was wearing a fancy new black dress, and she had ordered the finest of fine coffins for her brother. It had gold handles and a silk lining. Cass was wearing a fancy suit that he wouldn't have ever picked out for himself, and he looked kind of peaceful lying there. Everyone in the church said this was one fine funeral Addie Bell had put together for her little brother.

I felt mighty uncomfortable looking at all those decorations bought with the insurance money. I reckoned Cass would rather be wedding with Josephine than laid out in funeral splendor, but he didn't get a vote in the matter. Since the insurance doctor had signed his death certificate saying he died of indigestion, no one was going to drag Addie Bell to the courthouse and accuse her of murder. This wasn't right, but there wasn't anything I could do about it except pray the Lord would take care of it, somehow.

Well, the preacher took to preaching with such vigor that we were there for a full three hours hearing about how kind Cass had been and how beautiful Heaven was and how he'd be waiting there for his poor Josephine and his generous sister, Addie Bell, and how all the angels would be singing there before the good Lord. When the preacher finally wound down his sermon, he beckoned to Addie Bell to come up front among the heaped-up piles of flowers and ferns. She stood right beside Cass in his coffin and led the whole congregation in the last hymn, which was "Steal Away."

Addie Bell belted out the words in her fine mezzo-soprano. She gripped the side of the coffin with one hand and swayed back and forth like a sapling in a windstorm. And the congregation, they were singing and stomping with her, slow and solemn. By the second verse, the whole church was a-creaking and a-groaning until it sounded like it was mourning with us. And suddenly, the whole front of the church gave way. The rafters cracked and busted loose. The walls sagged inward, raining shingles on everyone in the front pews. The organ pitched forward, missing the pulpit and the coffin by a whisker and falling right smack dab on Addie Bell. For a tense second, everything was still, and I thought it might be over. Then the whole floor gave way. Organ, pulpit, coffin, and all plummeted eight feet down to the dirt floor below, and the rafters caved in above them.

When the coffin hit the floor of the cellar, Cass's body flew out. He landed against one of the posts that supported the floor, and there he sat with his dead eyes staring accusingly at Addie Bell and one arm flung straight out to point at the place where her body lay, squashed flat by the heavy organ. Nobody else was hurt.

After that, there was no question in anyone's mind that Addie Bell had poisoned her brother, Cass, to keep him from marrying Josephine Foxhall. And the Lord God Almighty had struck her dead for her meanness.

It was one fine funeral, sure enough. Folks in the neighborhood still talk about it to this day.

22

Stingy Jack

When the new preacher moved to town, the members of his new congregation were quick to tell him about Stingy Jack, the Jack-o'-Lantern that was haunting the old road through the swamp. But the new preacher didn't believe in Stingy Jack. He told his congregation that they were seeing some sort of mist or starlight reflected on the water. It was just their imagination, populating the shadows with ghosts and evil spirits.

The congregation listened closely to the new preacher and thought he might be right about Stingy Jack. Then again, he might be wrong, him being new to the area and all. So they kept turning their pockets inside out when they walked down the road through the swamp, because that was what a body was supposed to do to keep the Jack-o'-Lantern away. And most folks avoided the old road at night if they could. No use tempting fate.

At first the preacher treated the whole story like a joke. But as the months passed, he became more and more cross whenever he heard folks talking about the Jack-o'-Lantern. He'd give a little hop of rage if he saw anybody walking around with their pockets turned inside out. Seemed to him like they

STINGY JACK

were following heathen ways instead of trusting God to protect them from evil.

One Saturday evening, the preacher was reading his Bible out on the front porch when he saw Sister Margaret passing by with all her clothes inside out. Well, that did it! The next day, the preacher got up into the pulpit and announced to the whole congregation that he was going to walk the old swamp road that very night as the clock struck midnight, just to prove that the Jack-o'-Lantern didn't exist. When he got home in one piece, they were all to stop their heathen practices and trust in the Lord to protect them ever after.

The congregation exchanged worried looks with one another. "If you get home, you mean," muttered Brother Eustace. He thought he spoke soft enough, but the preacher heard him and glared at him from the pulpit, giving a little hop of rage and waving his Bible for emphasis.

After church, folks crowded round the preacher and tried to give him their lucky amulets and silver coins. But the preacher wouldn't take none of them heathen things.

"The Lord will protect me," he told them all. "The only thing I'm going to take is the Holy Book. When all of you come to the swamp road tomorrow morning, you'll see me walking out of the swamp with my head held high and my clothes right side out. Then you'll know that the Jack-o'-Lantern is just a fairy tale."

No one could talk the preacher out of his plan. The congregation went home, shaking their heads in sorrow. The preacher was a holy man of God, that was obvious. But Jack-o'-Lantern was pure evil. There was no telling who would win this contest. No telling at all.

The oldest of the stories said that Jack-o'-Lantern was once an evil man called Stingy Jack who made a lot of trouble for folks while he was alive. When he grew old, Stingy Jack played a trick on the Devil so he wouldn't go to Hell when he died. He caught the Devil in a trap and didn't free him until the Devil gave him another ten years of life and pledged not to take his soul at the end of them. The pledge backfired on Stingy Jack, because when it came time to die, the good Lord wouldn't let him into Heaven and the Devil wouldn't let him into Hell. Stingy Jack had no place to go. His eternal soul was forced to wander the earth, with only a single piece of brimstone to light his way. Stingy Jack was so bitter at this turn of events that he made his own pledge. He vowed to spend his days luring the good folks of this world to their death in the swamp, because they were going to Heaven and he was stuck on Earth.

Folks knew the preacher was tempting fate, trying to outwit an evil spirit like Stingy Jack. After all, this was a being who had outwitted the Devil himself. They reckoned the preacher didn't stand a chance against him, so the church deacons decided to camp out along the edge of the swamp that night so they'd be near enough to rescue their preacher in case Stingy Jack came for him.

On the stroke of midnight, the preacher walked into the swamp, just like he promised. He carried a walking stick to test for marshy spots, and under his arm he held his Bible. He had scouted out a fallen tree in the middle of the swamp that morning that he reckoned would make a good place to spend the night. He headed down a path toward his chosen spot, humming hymns to himself as he walked.

All at once, the preacher caught a glimpse of a light ahead of him. *Must be a reflection from the lantern at Sister Margaret's place,* he thought, not realizing that Sister Margaret's place was several miles away in the opposite direction.

The wind hissed through the tops of the trees along the path. It almost sounded like the words "Stin-gy Jack. Stin-gy Jack." The preacher shivered and pulled his jacket tight around him. *Autumn must come early in these parts,* he thought as he ventured deeper into the swamp.

It wasn't long before the earth started to wobble under the preacher's boots, and he had to use his walking stick to make sure the next step was solid before he took it. The wind whistled through the tall grass around him, swirling the blades this way and that. They wrapped around the preacher's arms and legs like the misty hands of a ghost. Somewhere deep in the swamp, a voice hissed: "Stin-gy Jack. Stin-gy Jack."

The preacher's hair stood on end. He shuddered, clutching his Bible to his chest and raising the walking stick like a weapon. A cold breeze swept down his neck and under his collar.

"This is nonsense," he muttered. "There's nobody here tonight but me and the Lord."

A light flickered somewhere off to the right. "Stin-gy Jack. Stin-gy Jack," a sinister voice hissed softly under the rustling of the wind in the grass.

The preacher was shaking so hard that the soggy ground under him made little splashing noises. "The Lord is with me!" he shouted. The sound disappeared within a few feet, but the words unlocked the preacher's frozen knees. He stepped forward carefully, prodding the ground with his stick and muttering the Lord's Prayer to himself as he walked.

Suddenly the wind died away and the sliver of moon disappeared behind a cloud. The swamp was plunged into blackness. An eerie silence wrapped around the preacher until the only thing he could hear was the slosh of watery ground under his boots and the sound of his own breath.

The preacher's heart started thumping fiercely. He wished—oh, how he wished—that he'd reached the fallen tree before night fell and had its firm trunk against his back. Anything could be out here with him—anything at all.

Suddenly the Jack-o'-Lantern stories didn't sound so ridiculous.

A light appeared on his right, lighting up a long, low pool of water filled with reeds. The light blinked on . . . off . . . on . . . off. "Stin-gy Jack," an evil voice hissed softly. "Stin-gy Jack."

The preacher fumbled for the pockets in his jacket and hastily turned them inside out. He felt guilty for doing such a heathen thing, but fear was foremost in his mind. Something was out here with him. Even with a Bible clutched to his chest, he didn't feel safe.

The preacher's knees knocked as he moved carefully through the swamp. He prayed loudly, hoping the holy words would deter whatever evil thing stalked him.

A light appeared. The preacher whirled to face it with a shriek. The light hovered over the soggy pathway, and bright little sparkles danced invitingly on the waters of a deep pool at the edge of the trail. The preacher raised his walking stick and shouted, "Go away, in the name of God!"

Directly behind him, a sinister voice hissed in his ear: "Stin-gy Jack. Stin-gy Jack."

Slivers of ice ran along the preacher's skin. He whirled round with a scream, slashing at his stalker with the walking stick. It passed right through the glowing, emaciated form looming on the path beside him. Stingy Jack's face was bone white, and his eyes were two glowing red coals.

"Stin-gy Jack. Stin-gy Jack," the spirit howled.

The preacher staggered backward, tripped over a weedy hummock, and nearly pitched headlong into the deep pool. He was saved when his jacket caught on a splinter of wood sticking out from a rotting stump beside the water. He yanked himself free just as the ghost light faded, leaving the path in darkness. The preacher gasped in panic. The Jack-o'-Lantern could be anywhere. Anywhere! But if he ran, he'd fall into a pool and drown!

"Stin-gy Jack. Stin-gy Jack," hissed a sinister voice right above his head.

The preacher pulled off his jacket and turned it inside out, just as a bright light burst into being directly above his head. Crouching by the stump, the preacher opened his Bible and covered his face with it. He felt ghostly hands plucking at his body. The touch was so cold it burnt his skin, right through his clothes.

"Stin-gy Jack. Stin-gy Jack," hissed the Jack-o'-Lantern.

"The Lord will protect me!" the preacher screamed from underneath the Bible plastered against his face. "The Lord will protect me!"

A rumble of wagon wheels answered his cry. Blazing torches lit the path as the church deacons came running to save their preacher. The ghost light vanished as they swarmed the place where the preacher crouched beside a dark pool. The searchers tried to rouse the trembling preacher, but he lay under his Bible in a stupor of terror. He wouldn't move. The men were forced to carry him down the swamp path and out to the road, where they tucked him into the back of the wagon with the hay bales.

When he woke hours later, the preacher babbled madly about ghosts and evil spirits and glowing red eyes. He tore all his clothes off and tried unsuccessfully to turn them inside out. It took several men to restrain him. The doctor was forced to sedate the preacher to make him sleep again.

In the end, the preacher was sent to a home for the insane. Every day for the rest of his life, he babbled to the attendants about the evil Jack-o'-Lantern and screamed every time he saw a bright light.

These days, no one remembers the old road that once passed through the swamp. It's completely overgrown, and the new road avoids the spot where the preacher met Stingy Jack. Which is a mercy.

23

Psychology

In the 1890s or thereabouts, there was a story going around these parts about a famous spiritualist who could get rid of haints from just about any place he wanted. He told everyone that he used "psychology" to get rid of ghosts, and it worked every time. I'd never heard the word "psychology" before, but a university fellow told me it meant the ghost buster figured out what was going on in the minds of the haints, and then he fixed it so they didn't want to haint a place no more.

Now, this spiritualist was traveling through Sevier County when he came upon an old church that had been abandoned due to haints. The church would have been real pretty if'n it was taken care of, but by now the shingles were falling off, the weeds had grown up around the yard, bushes had crowded the walls, and vines grew every which way over the building. The sanctuary itself was all cracked windows and dust and cobwebs. Folks reckoned that haints from the graveyard took over the place once the congregation got careless with their finances and stopped caring for the building. It was a durn shame.

The spiritualist went to the mayor of the town and said he reckoned he could get rid of the ghosts in that church if folks

PSYCHOLOGY

were interested. So the mayor talked it over with the preacher, who was holding services in people's houses 'cause the church was hainted, and they told the spiritualist they'd be much obliged if he'd free the building from the haints.

"How you going to do it, mister?" asked the mayor. "I reckon there's too many of the haints for a body to do it all on his own."

"You just have to know what makes them tick," the spiritualist said mysteriously. "Psychology . . . "

Well, the preacher gathered his congregation together and they all knelt down in the yard in front of the abandoned church and had them a big prayer meeting, blessing the spiritualist six ways to Sunday in the hope that he'd come back alive after facing them haints.

It was dusky dark by the time everyone who wanted to finished praying over the man. Finally, the spiritualist raised up from his knees, shook hands with the mayor, the preacher, and a couple of deacons. Then he marched up the steps to the front door of the church.

A couple of the sisters broke down weeping, and a very pretty single lady who had taken a shine to the spiritualist begged him not to go in. But the spiritualist was determined to face down those haints. So he opened the door and stepped inside the haunted building—and the only tools he took with him were his gumption and his psychology.

As soon as he closed the door, the air in the church turned stone-cold. A small breeze swept round about his body, looking him over like a curious cat. The spiritualist heard something rattling against the windows like old bones scraping glass. The hairs prickled on the back of his neck as he sensed eyes watching his every move.

The spiritualist reckoned he should set down for a moment and get his bearings, so he moved cautiously forward until he reached the back pew. The rising moon glowed through the fancy stained-glass window behind the pulpit, casting colored shadows around the sanctuary. He strained his eyes, looking here and there for the haints he felt watching him as he groped for a seat on the back bench.

When he sat down, his hand landed in a sticky wet pool of something. The spiritualist glanced to his left and saw an old, old deacon sitting there beside him. His skin was glowing from the inside out, and his body was split nearly in half so that blood was gushing over his Sunday suit and down into the pew. The spiritualist's hand had landed in the haint's open wound, and silvery blood covered it from palm to fingertip! His whole body shuddered and shook with the shock of it.

"Don't ye get excited, son," the old deacon haint whispered. His voice sounded like dried leaves rattling in the wind. "This is all for a cause."

"I'm mighty glad to hear it," the spiritualist said, raising himself off that pew and stepping away. His knees were trembling so much he could hardly walk, but he wanted to put some distance between himself and that haint. It was difficult to do psychology when his hand was dripping with phantom blood.

The spiritualist sidled backward, his eyes fixed on the dead deacon bleeding in the last pew. This time he put his right hand behind him, feeling for the bench across the aisle. His fingers closed on something boney instead. The spiritualist whipped his head around and saw two skeletons standing behind him. He nearly jumped out of his own skin when he saw the haints. The church folks had been right to pray for him. This was the most hainted place the spiritualist had ever seen! Still, his psychology had never failed him, so he tipped his hat politely to the phantoms and stepped lively up the aisle, heading toward the pulpit.

Just before he reached the first pew, five skeletons came a marching up the side aisle. They turned the corner sharply and lined up in front of the pulpit, blocking the spiritualist's way. He was a clever fellow, so he edged sideways, got a foot onto the bench of the front pew, and leapt clean over the line of skeletons.

The spiritualist landed in the fancy chair set on one side of the pulpit and found himself sitting on the lap of an old, old preacher who'd been dead more than a hundred years. The spiritualist let out a yell of surprise. His heart was pounding so hard he thought he'd keel over from fright. He jumped up at once and stammered an apology to the ancient haint. The dead preacher waved a shining hand and said, "Don't take on so, son. This is all for a cause."

This was all for a cause.

The phrase made the spiritualist stop in his tracks. Two different phantoms had said the same thing to him. It was time for the spiritualist to use some psychology and figure out what they meant.

The skeletons in the front aisle started shaking and rattling and chattering their teeth at the spiritualist. They swarmed up to the pulpit and pushed him back until his shoulders were against the altar. The spiritualist looked left and right, trying to find a way to escape the skeletons, and his eye landed on two big old collection bowls lying on a table beside the dead preacher. It gave him an idea. He looked into two glowing blue eyes, and the preacher haint winked at him. The spiritualist winked back. He had figured out what the deacon and the preacher were trying to tell him. They were using psychology on him! And he'd use psychology to get himself out of this mess.

The skeletons were pressing all around him, gripping him with bony hands. More and more appeared, until skeletal haints filled every pew in the church. The spiritualist shuffled backward toward the old preacher sitting by the table. He elbowed the skeletons around him quite rudely, forcing them to give way. They rattled their dry bones at him and snapped their teeth in irritation. Just two more steps. One more step. Got 'em!

The spiritualist grabbed the cobweb-covered collection plates and thrust them out in front of him. Addressing the skeletons in the pews, he said, "You ought to be ashamed of yourselves, letting this church get into such a terrible state. If you're going to haint it, you're going to pay to fix it up. I'm taking up a collection tonight, and I'm expecting every one of you to contribute generously to this cause."

The skeletons in the pews looked at one another in alarm. The spiritualist repressed a grin. Dead or alive, nobody wanted to spend money on something they'd been getting for free.

Turning to the skeletons surrounding the altar, he said, "Now, which of you dry bones are going to be my ushers?" The skeletons gazed at one another, eye socket to eye socket. Then they started vanishing, one by one, with a sound like a cork pulled out of a bottle.

Pop, pop, pop, pop. In a moment, they were all gone.

"Guess I'll have to do the ushering myself," the spiritualist said, and stepped forward with the collection plates. He offered one to the skeleton sitting in the first pew. The skeleton reeled back and vanished with a pop. The spiritualist looked at the next skeleton. It shook its head and vanished too. Once again, the air was suddenly filled with popping noises as alarmed skeletons vanished from the sanctuary.

In under a minute, the haints were all gone.

From his seat behind the altar, the old preacher laughed in triumph. In the back pew, the old deacon cried "Hallelujah." Then both ghosts vanished in a glitter of blue light.

The church was plunged into darkness once more.

The spiritualist tapped the two collection plates against each other thoughtfully. Psychology told him that he had to take one more step to keep all the haints from coming back to the church. He marched down the aisle and out to the yard, where the mayor and the preacher were waiting for him. The spiritualist handed each man a collection plate.

"The haints are all gone," he said, "at least for now. But they will come back, I reckon, unless you fix the place up, sanctify it, and start using it for your worship services. The only reason those haints took over in the first place was because the congregation stopped taking care of the building."

"It was already hainted when I was called to serve here," the preacher protested weakly.

The spiritualist just eyed him, letting psychology do the work.

"I suppose I could have encouraged the congregation to clean the place up instead of abandoning it completely," he admitted after a painful silence.

The spiritualist dug into his pocket and pulled out a dollar. "Here's my contribution to the cause."

"But we should be paying you," protested the mayor.

"Never mind. It's all for the cause," said the spiritualist. He winked at the ghost of the old preacher, who had shimmered into existence among the shadows behind the mayor.

The new preacher saw the haint and gulped in alarm.

"If you use psychology, you'll have plenty of funds for the church," the spiritualist told the two men. "You'll have it fixed up in no time."

With a nod, he strode out of the churchyard and went on his way.

The next time the spiritualist traveled through Sevier County, he stopped by on a Sunday morning to see what had happened with the old church. The spiritualist was pleased to see that the church was fixed up like new. The pews were filled to bursting with congregants. They were singing hymns and contributing liberally to the collection plate. It was as close to Heaven as you could get in this old world.

All on account of psychology.

24

Apple Cobbler

GREAT SMOKY MOUNTAINS

Back in the day, when you heard about a cow falling sick or someone having real bad luck with hunting, you knew the family had a problem with witches. Witches could give you the jerks at night so that you cried out in pain in your sleep. They messed with the milk so it was bloody or it wouldn't churn or the cow dried up completely. They could turn themselves into black cats and sneak around watching folks. They could transform a person into a horse and ride you. And sometimes they'd kill a body outright if you inconvenienced them in any way.

I know this for a fact, on account of it happened to my first cousin once removed. Here's her story.

Folks were a-feared of my cousin's youngest girl, Sary. She was as heartless and selfish as they came. If Sary couldn't get her way as a babe, she'd throw a fit so bad that her ma and pa thought she'd hurt herself. So they gave in to her when they should have stood firm. Just about the only body who could make Sary mind as a young'un was her elder sister, Anne. And, boy howdy, did Sary hate her on account of it.

When Sary was older, she started bossing all of her younger cousins around. If they wouldn't do what she told them, she'd

Apple Cobbler

try to get them in trouble with their folks. Took a while, but their parents finally figured out what Sary was doing and told her to stop it.

Sary sulked for a whole month after folks caught on to her tricks. Then she did something awful. I wouldn't have believed it if I hadn't seen it with my own eyes. One night after prayer meeting, she went down to the crossroads and made a deal with the devil. I was coon hunting that night, and when I saw a lantern flickering on the road, I was curious and went to see what's what. And there was Sary, standing in front of a dark figure with horns on his head and cloven feet, and she was swearing to serve him if he'd let her have her way with folks. She patted her head and her foot, saying everything in between belonged to the devil, and then she cut her finger, dropped her blood into a book, and repeated some strange words that the devil told her to say in a magic language that made my eyes water. When the devil looked over Sary's head and straight into the place I was hiding in the bushes, I skedaddled right out of there, scared to death.

I slept with the Bible under my pillow that night. In the morning, I put a circle of salt around my cabin and hung a broom across my door, which is supposed to keep witches out. Then I thought so long my brain started hurting, trying to figure out how to tell my cousin her youngest daughter was a witch. I knew she wouldn't believe me if I came right out and said it. She'd say I'd been drinking moonshine and made the whole thing up. I finally decided I'd wait and see if Sary started witching folks. Maybe she'd change her mind and go to the preacher to get herself fixed.

Sary began practicing her magic right away. She started with small, mean things. School classmates who annoyed her had bad luck. The boys' britches would rip when they bent over, or they'd drop the ball when they were playing games at recess. The girls would get headaches or lose their homework or something embarrassing would happen in front of a boy they liked. They were nasty little things, but nothing dangerous.

But when Sary witched the girl who was her chief rival at school, I knew I had to say something to my cousin. The girl's favorite cow stopped giving milk, and no amount of doctoring would fix her up. The cow stopped eating and finally laid down and wouldn't get up again. They had to shoot it. It broke the poor girl's heart because she raised that cow all on her own. Folks figured it must be a witch that done it, but no one imagined the witch was Sary.

My cousin wouldn't listen when I told her what I'd seen that night at the crossroads. "Sary would never do something like that," she told me and accused me of drinking too much moonshine, just like I thought she would. At least I'd warned her.

I was real concerned when Sary started pulling tricks on her sister. Anne was the eldest daughter in the family, and she'd been caring for her younger sisters and brothers as long as I can remember. Sary hated her big sister because Anne made her mind her manners. She wouldn't let Sary get away with any nonsense, even when Sary turned the whole house upside down with her tantrums. So Anne became Sary's next target.

Food would disappear off Anne's plate and reappear on Sary's. Anne lost weight because she wasn't getting enough to eat. Then Anne started falling off the bed she shared with Sary. Their pa built a rail to keep her in, and she still ended up on the floor every night. They finally moved her to another room, and Sary had the big bed all to herself.

Anne started tripping over invisible objects when she was walking to school. She would fall flat on her face in front of her friends, which embarrassed her terribly. Once, she plunged down the bank of the river and would have been swept away and drowned if her brother hadn't jumped into the water to rescue her.

My heart jumped into my throat when I heard that story. I knew then that Sary wasn't going to stop until her sister was dead, so I took Anne aside and warned her about Sary's new powers and what they meant. Anne took the news calmly. I figured she didn't believe me any more than her ma had. Anne was too polite to say I'd been drinking, but I could tell she wasn't going to take precautions against Sary's witching.

Come autumn, my cousin's apple orchard was filled to overflowing with fruit. I'd been invited to have supper with the family and was chatting with my cousin in the kitchen when Anne came in and begged her mother to make some apple cobbler for supper. My cousin smiled and said, "Go on then, girl, and get some apples for me to cook with."

"I don't want apple cobbler," Sary said from her seat by the window. "You leave those apples alone, Anne."

"Don't eat the apple cobbler, then," my cousin said to her youngest. "But the rest of us will enjoy it. You go on, Anne. Pick me a sack of apples, and I'll do you a crumble for supper."

So Anne got a sack and headed out to the orchard to fetch the apples for her ma. Sary caught up with her just as she reached the path through the laurel bushes and said, "The Dark Man will get you, Anne, for taking them apples."

"Don't talk nonsense, Sary," Anne said briskly, and started down the trail to the orchard.

When she got to the apple trees, she walked all around with her sack, picking ripe apples from the lower branches and from the ground until her sack was full. As she worked, she saw movement out of the corner of her eye, but whenever she looked this way or that, nothing was there.

Her sack was almost full when she reached for one last perfect apple hanging almost out of reach—and found herself eye-to-eye with a racoon. The critter climbed right down the branch and stood blocking the apple. It made Anne uneasy. She'd never seen a racoon act that way before. When the coon bared its teeth at her, she decided she had more than enough apples to make cobbler and stepped away from the tree.

Anne shouldered the sack of apples and started back for home. As she walked, she saw racoons looking at her from up in the trees, from among the laurel, and from the side of the path. It was strange to see so many coons in one area. They were standing silent and still. Watching her.

Anne picked up her pace, trying to get away from the staring eyes. She'd never taken my story of Sary at the crossroads seriously, but she was having second thoughts now. When she reached the clearing where the family cabin stood, she felt something tugging on the front of her dress. She looked down and saw that her way was blocked by a line of racoons, stretching from one side of the clearing to the other. The critters closest to her stood on their hind legs and were gripping the fabric of her skirt in their claws.

Anne gasped in fear. She glanced frantically around and saw racoons on her left, on her right, and filling the path behind her. She was surrounded.

"Get away from me," she screamed, grabbing her skirt with her free hand and yanking it away from the coons. She kicked frantically at the critters blocking her way and managed to fling them off her dress. She ran as fast as she could, yelling and flapping her free hand at the racoons, who kept pace with her, front, back, and sides. They kept throwing themselves at Anne as she ran. Some climbed the fence and leapt onto her head and shoulders, tearing at her with their teeth and raking her with their claws.

My cousin and I heard Anne screaming from the house. We looked out the window and saw a mass of black-and-gray fur, filling the whole yard. It looked as if Sary had summoned every raccoon in the Great Smokies to the farm. The racoons were nipping at Anne's heels and taking bites out of her face, her hands, her arms, her legs. Anywhere they could reach.

I grabbed my cousin's rifle and started shooting, but there were too many of them, and I couldn't aim anywhere close to Anne for fear of hitting her. My cousin grabbed rocks from the ground and threw them into the roiling mass of striped tails and gray-and-black fur, but it was like trying to drain the ocean with a spoon. It wasn't enough.

Anne put on a final burst of speed and leapt across the threshold. We slammed the door behind her, and she fell screaming to the floor. The sack fell from her shoulder and burst open, apples rolling everywhere.

As soon as she entered the cabin, the mass of racoons vanished into the woods on either side of the field, except one that still clung to Anne's skirts. My cousin made quick work of it, ripping it off and breaking its neck with the twist she usually reserved for killing chickens.

Anne was desperately injured. There was no way we could reach a doc in time to fix her. She was bleeding out from too many bites, and a vein in her neck was cut clean through. She gasped out the story to me and my cousin, her blood staining our clothes and pooling around the apples scattered across the floor. Then her eyes rolled back and she died with a shudder. My cousin screamed in agony and fell weeping across her eldest daughter's body.

A shadow crossed my face. I looked up and saw Sary standing in the doorway, a packed satchel held in her hand.

"I told you I don't like apple cobbler," she said. Then she walked away—out of the clearing and out of our lives. We never saw her again.

A few years ago, I heard a story about a witch who lived a couple of mountaintops away in North Carolina. The way the fellow described the woman made me think of Sary. I didn't tell my cousin. I figured she'd suffered enough, losing her eldest and youngest daughters on the same day. But I wondered.

25

Churning Butter

CUMBERLAND GAP

Back in the old days, before electric lights and such, a man named Harold lived with his pretty wife, Mary Ann, on a small farm way back in the mountains of Tennessee. They were a happy couple, with two grown children and nice neighbors and livestock enough to keep body and soul together.

One day Harold went over to see his neighbor, hoping to trade with him for a few hogs. When Harold reached the neighbor's house, the wife came to the door and told Harold that her husband was out in the fields. The wife invited Harold inside to wait for her husband.

Harold sat down and waited patiently while his neighbor's wife started churning butter. She churned faster and faster until the churn was brimming with butter. Harold was amazed. Mary Ann couldn't churn butter like that. There must be some kind of trick to it, Harold decided.

Wanting to get to the bottom of the mystery, Harold asked his neighbor's wife if she would get him a drink. As soon as she went out the door with her bucket, he examined her churn. It looked the same as his wife's churn. Then Harold looked underneath it. There was a small black rag under the churn.

CHURNING BUTTER

It looked like a piece had been cut from an old dress. Harold clipped off a corner of the rag, put the churn back exactly as the woman had left it, and sat down.

After drinking a dipper of water, Harold told his neighbor's wife that he was going to try to find her man out in the fields. Wishing her a good day, Harold hurried out of the house. But instead of looking for his neighbor, Harold went home to his wife.

"Mary, I need you to do some churning," he called as soon as he entered the house.

"But Harold, we've already got more butter than we need. And there's almost no cream left for churning," Mary Ann answered, looking surprised by his request.

But Harold insisted that Mary Ann churn the rest of the cream immediately. Mary Ann knew her husband pretty well, and she knew he was up to something. But it was no use trying to figure it out when he was in this mood, so she got out her churn and put in the last of the cream.

"Before you start, Mary, why don't I put this bit of black rag under your churn?" said Harold, taking the rag out of his pocket. Mary Ann looked at him suspiciously, but she let him place the black rag under her churn and then began working the cream. To her astonishment, she could feel the churn filling with butter, even though there hadn't been enough cream in it to make more than a dab. And her arms were moving twice as fast as normal.

Mary Ann began to feel frightened because the butter was coming faster and in greater quantities than it ever should. She jumped up, grabbed her churn, and shouted, "I don't know what devilment you're up to, Harold, but I won't be a part of it." She ran out the door and dumped the bewitched butter in the woods.

Harold grabbed up the bit of black rag and stuffed it in his pocket. He felt bad about scaring his wife, and decided he would apologize to her as soon as he finished his evening chores.

Harold was just heading back to the house after the milking was done when he came face-to-face with a large figure that looked something like a man, except it had a small pair of horns on its head. The sun seemed to glow red around the figure, which Harold found mighty strange, because the sun had already set behind the mountaintop. Harold stopped dead and looked into the tall figure's burning black eyes. The figure bowed and held out a book to Harold, saying, "Sign here, please."

"What do you mean, sign here? Sign for what? If you want me to sign that book, you've gotta hand it to me," Harold snapped. He was mighty nervous of that glowing figure with the horns.

"I can't come over to you," the horned figure said.

Harold saw that there was a glowing circle surrounding his body, which stopped a few inches from the horned figure. Harold was frightened, but he reached over and took the book. When he opened it, he saw writing at the top of the first page: "We and All We Possess Belong to The Devil." This was followed by the names of all his neighbors. At the top of the list was the name of the neighbor woman who had the black rag under her churn.

Harold looked over at the horned figure. It was glaring at him with flaming eyes. Harold was scared nearly to death, but he said, "I'm not signing this. I don't belong to the devil and neither do my wife and children."

"That seems strange to me," said the horned figure, his eyes glowing brighter with each word. "You've been using witchcraft. What about that black rag you put under your churn?"

Harold felt the rag twitch in his pocket, then a little black bird came flying out and landed on his wrist. The bird gave a horrible chuckle. It sounded like a demon. And so it was. It gave a second chuckle and flew over to perch on the shoulder of the horned figure.

Harold knew he had to do something quickly. He turned the page over, wrote "We and All We Possess Belong to The Lord," and signed his name to the page. Then he handed the book back. The horned figure took one look at the book and gave a terrible, piercing scream before bursting into flames, smoke swirling around and around it. There was a bright flash and a smell of brimstone, and Harold fell onto the ground as the horned figure disappeared.

As soon as Harold got back on his feet, he ran right to the house and told Mary Ann the whole story.

"We're not staying here another day," Harold said. "I won't stay in a place where all my neighbors have sold themselves to the devil."

Harold and Mary Ann packed up and left the next day. Their children and their families also left after hearing Harold's story. There's no one living on that side of the hill anymore, just a few abandoned buildings and a burned spot where nothing will grow. Folks reckon that's the spot where the horned figure stood when it tried to get Harold to sign its book. Everyone around these parts calls that spot "the devil's place," and no one goes there.

26

Jimmy Lonesome

RHEA COUNTY

When I heard they left old Jimmy Lonesome in the upstairs room of the old courthouse after Doc retired, I knew it would cause trouble. Jimmy Lonesome was the old skeleton Doc kept on display in his office. Old bones don't like to be left unburied, and Jimmy Lonesome had been in Doc's office for as long as I can remember.

The first time I saw Jimmy Lonesome was in 1869, the day Ma took me to see the Doc because of a putrid throat. I was five years old, and when I saw the skeleton standing in the corner of the office, I almost ran away. Blue light flashed briefly in the skeleton's vacant eye sockets when I stepped in the room, but it vanished before I could show Ma. I felt Jimmy Lonesome staring at me from the moment I entered Doc's office to the moment I left. It made my skin crawl.

I asked Doc why he kept the skeleton in his workplace. Didn't he know the story of Raw Head and Bloody Bones? The old bones in that story were a heap of trouble, and Jimmy Lonesome seemed like he might be a Raw Head in the making. Doc laughed and said Raw Head was an old granny's tale. Doc believed in science, not superstition. He told me Jimmy

JIMMY LONESOME

Lonesome was a nice man who donated his body to science when he died. He wouldn't hurt a fly. Me, I wasn't so sure.

I was a man myself now, studying for my university exam, and I too believed more in science than superstition. But I still had a funny feeling whenever I thought about Jimmy Lonesome. Doc was moving south to live with his married daughter, and she didn't want to share her fine house with a skeleton, so Jimmy Lonesome was left in the upstairs corner room, standing by the window and gathering dust.

Now, the county used to rent out the upstairs rooms in the old courthouse—one to Doc and the rest to a couple who ran it as a lodge. One night, a lodger named Peterson went missing. They found him shot to death in Doc's old office. No one knew who did it. The only witness to the crime was Jimmy Lonesome, and the skeleton wasn't talking. After the incident, the couple shut down the lodge and the upstairs of the courthouse was left vacant, except for Jimmy Lonesome. A month or so later, strange things started happening at the courthouse.

Judge Locke was catching up on some paperwork in his office one night after everyone else had left when he heard footsteps walking swiftly overhead. They started in the corner where Jimmy Lonesome stood in the corner window and hurried across to the door on the far side. Then he heard a loud thud, as if a big box had dropped on the floor. The sound was so loud that his ceiling reverberated with the noise.

The judge charged upstairs to confront the intruder and eject him from the premises. No one was there. Jimmy Lonesome stood alone next to the window, his empty eye sockets gazing innocently at the judge. The judge went to the window and tested it. It was locked, and the glass was intact. Then he went

179

through the rest of the upstairs, checking for trespassers and testing windows. No one was there. Puzzled, he returned to his office to finish up the paperwork so he could go home to his dinner.

The footsteps and the jarring noise happened again the next night, and the next. Each time the judge investigated the sounds, he found everything locked up tight. It was frustrating, to say the least. The fourth or fifth time it happened, the judge marched into the corner room and said, "Stop messing around, Jimmy Lonesome!" That seemed to calm things down somewhat. The incidents slowed to once a week.

"I don't know if it's Peterson's ghost or if Jimmy Lonesome is just looking for some company," the judge confided to me one evening over a beer at the tavern. "But something's haunting the upstairs of the courthouse."

Remembering the blue flash I'd seen in the eye sockets of the skeleton when I was a boy, I could well believe it.

While I was away at university, there was another incident in the courthouse. A fellow named Burkett was starting his first law practice in town, and he was as poor as a church mouse. To save money, he obtained permission to sleep in the little corner room where Jimmy Lonesome stood watch in the window. Judge Locke warned him about the ghostly footsteps, but Burkett said he didn't mind.

The first night Burkett stayed in the room, he clearly heard footsteps walking across to the door and then back again, but he could see nothing at all. The footsteps marched straight up to the bed, and he felt something looking down on him. Shivers ran up and down his spine, and Burkett put his head under the pillow and kept it there until the feeling of being watched went away. He didn't get much sleep that night.

Deciding that he wouldn't let a few phantom footsteps stand between himself and a free place to stay, Burkett returned to the haunted room the next evening. He was almost asleep when he heard phantom footsteps marching across the floor. This time, they came straight toward his cot. A moment later, a pair of skeletal hands seized Burkett, jerked him out of the bed, covers and all, and threw him out the door. A moment later, the pillow followed him. Burkett didn't wait for the rest of the cot. With a shriek of terror, he pounded down the staircase and out the front door of the courthouse. He ran all the way to the inn in his nightshirt and begged the innkeeper to let him sleep in a corner of the bar for the rest of the night.

Burkett refused to go back into the courthouse the next morning, so Judge Locke had to retrieve his belongings from the upstairs room. Burkett left town that morning, declaring his intention of starting his practice in the next county so he'd never have to argue a case in the haunted courthouse.

Burkett's story was discussed with great interest all over town. There was some debate over the identity of the ghost. Was it Peterson or Jimmy Lonesome causing all the ruckus? No one knew for sure.

The antics of the ghost in the courthouse continued off and on the whole time I was studying at university. When I returned to my hometown with my own law degree, my mother entertained me with stories about Jimmy Lonesome and the various clerks, officers, and attorneys who'd encountered him. The most striking was the tale of a young officer who accidentally started a fire when a piece of cloth drifted down from a decaying curtain and landed on the hot stovepipe that ran through the upper story and out the ceiling. The officer saw the flames lighting the stairwell and ran upstairs to stomp out the fire before the building burned. Once the fire was out, he climbed the ladder to the cupola, following the stovepipe to its point of egress to make sure nothing else flammable was attached to it. Satisfied that all was well, he groped his way down the ladder into the darkness below, having failed to bring a lantern or even a match with him in his rush to put out the fire.

As he set foot on the second floor, a voice called: "Is the fire all out?"

"I think so," he replied. Then he felt a chill pass over his skin, for the voice came out of the air in front of him, but there was no one else in the building at the time. That was the last time the officer ever went upstairs in the courthouse.

I started work the next morning as a clerk to Judge Locke. He asked if I minded working upstairs, since the first floor was filled to overflowing with courthouse staff. I considered for a moment, remembering the stories about Jimmy Lonesome and the haunted room. Then I said yes. Why not? The ghostly occurrences had all happened after dark. It should be safe enough upstairs during the day.

I sat at the desk they set up in the main room, reading and making notes for most of the day. By early evening, I was surrounded by stacks of files and books. They were piled haphazardly on the desk, on the extra chair, and even on the floor. My head was spinning with all the things I needed to know for my new position.

I went to the inn for a bite of dinner then hurried back to the courthouse to retrieve a book I wanted to study that night. I lit a lantern and walked up the steps to my impromptu second-floor office. Setting the lantern on the desk, I rifled through the stack of books on the floor, looking for the one I needed. Just as my fingers closed over it, the room around me filled with blue light, as bright as noonday. Gathering my courage, I looked up. Jimmy Lonesome loomed over me, a blue candle hovering over his skull and twin blue lights glowing in his eye sockets.

"Good evening, Jimmy. It's nice to see you again," I squeaked.

The skeleton cocked his head to the right, as if evaluating my statement for its veracity.

I rocked back on my heels and stammered, "My mother's expecting me soon, so I'd best be off. See you tomorrow!"

I scrambled backward on hands and feet until I'd put a good yard between us. Then I leapt up, tucked the book under my arm, and grabbed the lantern from the desk.

"Good night!" I gabbled and bolted for the stairs, jumping over the last few steps to the first floor.

Judge Locke peered out the door to his office as I thundered past.

"Jimmy Lonesome?" he called.

"Jimmy Lonesome," I agreed, sliding to a halt and stepping into his doorway. I was breathless from my rapid descent. "I m . . . may need to move my desk downstairs."

"Or you could take your books with you when you go to dinner," the judge countered.

"Good point," I conceded. "I can do that. Things were okay during the day. But Jimmy seems to need his space after hours."

"That he does," the judge said. "Don't stay up too late studying. I'll see you in the morning."

Dismissed, I hurried out the front door, then paused on the street and looked up at the corner window. I could barely make out the skeletal figure standing there. Then a little blue light sprang up over the skull and I could see Jimmy Lonesome gazing down at me. I waved my book in greeting and then headed for home.

27

Lovers' Lane

MARYVILLE

Everyone in my school grew up hearing the story of Skinned Tom. Kids told the story around Halloween, parents used it to warn us away from the lovers' lane when we hit puberty, and so on. It was *the* legend to tell anyone on their first visit to East Tennessee.

According to the story, Tom was a handsome fellow who lived in East Tennessee back in the 1920s. He was a rogue with a smooth manner that turned a lot of women's heads. Tom was a traveling salesman, a real love-them-and-leave-them sort. He'd swoop into a new town and sweet-talk all the eligible girls, and some not-so-eligible too, if you get my drift. Tom's ardor was intense while he pursued a girl. He'd sweep her off her feet with kisses and flowers, candy and false promises. But once he won her heart, he dropped her like a hotcake and started chasing the next girl in line. Folks claimed he bewitched the girls with some kind of charm. And it certainly seemed that way. The girls would walk around in a daze, falling into daydreams right in the middle of a conversation.

Of course Tom was as unpopular with the fellows and fathers as he was popular with the girls. There was usually a string of

LOVERS' LANE

last-minute weddings shortly after Tom left town. Many a bouncing baby that followed in the wake of these impromptu matrimonies looked more like Tom than the man who married the girl.

All the bad karma came home to roost the day Tom met a lovely married woman we will call "Geraldine." Now Geraldine prided herself on being a virtuous wife and a good mother. But none of that mattered once Tom came courting. The more she spurned his advances, the more persuasive he grew. Geraldine found herself yearning for things she shouldn't.

It didn't take long before the two started meeting "accidentally" in shops and restaurants and then taking rides in Tom's fancy motorcar. They became very well acquainted with all the remote places around town, but their favorite place to canoodle was the local lovers' lane.

It wasn't long before they were spotted by the very worst gossip in town, who went straight to Geraldine's husband to tell all. Now Geraldine's husband was the trusting sort, and he just could not believe that his wife would betray him. He was determined to witness the truth for himself before confronting his wayward wife. So he invented a business trip that would take him out of town for a week. Then he checked into a local hotel and kept watch on his wife, following her wherever she went. Once the children were safely packed off to school, it wasn't long before Tom arrived in his fancy motorcar and Geraldine tripped out merrily to meet him.

Geraldine's husband was devastated. He followed the couple at a distance and saw Tom park the car in the local lovers' lane and turn toward Geraldine with an amorous eye. At once, his sorrow turned to a terrible rage that made the world go blood red at the edges of his vision. He slammed out of his truck, stalked over to the car, and jerked open the driver's door. Untangling Tom from his wife, he threw the salesman from the car while his Geraldine desperately begged for mercy.

When her gaze met that of her husband, Geraldine realized he was too far gone for mercy. She flung herself out the passenger side door and fled half-clothed into the woods. Behind her, Tom screamed for mercy as Geraldine's husband pulled a hunting knife from his belt and started surgically slicing off his skin, one long strip at a time. Tom's screams became muted and ceased long before the husband was through. He tossed the bloody but still-breathing salesman on the ground and draped the man's skin on the open car door. Then he marched into the woods to look for Geraldine.

Later that evening, Geraldine's husband turned himself in to the police for murder and sent them to the lovers' lane to retrieve the bodies of Tom and Geraldine. When they arrived, they found blood everywhere and Tom's skin hanging from the open car door. A quick search revealed Geraldine in the woods nearby. She was bleeding from several knife wounds but miraculously still alive. But Tom's skinless body had disappeared.

Ever since that day, the spirit of Skinned Tom has stalked all the local lovers' lanes in East Tennessee, seeking out cheating couples and dismembering them with the same knife that was once welded against himself.

Now, I wasn't thinking about Skinned Tom or much of anything but romance on the night Justine and I parked the car in a secluded lane on the outskirts of town. I'd met her at a bar, and we'd been flirting outrageously for more than a week. When she suggested going for a drive, I knew what she wanted. And I had no objections. If things worked out the way I planned, I'd soon be taking Ms. Justine home to meet the folks. She was totally my type.

We were just getting cozy when someone thumped the back of the car so hard it shook. There were no lights in that dark lane, and no headlights had passed us coming or going.

"What is that? Is it a bear?" Justine gasped, pulling away from me and looking in alarm out the back window.

From outside the car, I caught a wisp of song: *Have you seen the ghost of Skinned Tom? Long white bones with the skin all gone . . .*

"It better not be some eavesdropping local kid," I muttered, flustered and disoriented by the interruption and the eerie chant still wafting faintly through the closed window.

I was straightening my clothes when my door was jerked open and I was thrown from the car by an icy wind. I rolled over just in time to avoid being stabbed with a hunting knife. I gazed up at a gruesome, skinless figure that glowed with a fiery light as it slashed at me with its knife. I screamed.

Justine was suddenly beside me, pulling me upright and shouting at the ghost of Skinned Tom: "I'm getting a divorce, all right? It will be finalized in the morning. *He didn't know!*"

She pepper-sprayed the ghost, but Skinned Tom didn't even blink. He took another swing with the knife, which seemed much too solid to be supernatural. We didn't wait around. Flinging ourselves into the car, we peeled out of the lovers' lane so fast we could smell the tires.

When we were safely in the parking lot behind my building, I looked over at Justine. She was pale and shaking with nerves. "I should have told you about the divorce," she gasped. "I never thought making out with you would trigger the ghost of Skinned Tom. I should have known better. My granny warned me long ago that there was an evil spirit haunting the area and that it became enraged when anyone was caught philandering in its sphere."

"I didn't think it was real," I said. My voice sounded too high-pitched to belong to me, but it reflected how I felt. "Thanks for saving me back there."

"I think maybe we should wait until my divorce is final before we . . . you know," Justine said.

"I agree," I said. "Can I drive you home?

"I'd like that. Thank you," she said primly. We held hands as I drove, and I gave her a chaste kiss on the cheek at her door.

Back in my apartment, I realized that I owed my aunt an apology letter. She'd been right to fear the ghost of Skinned Tom. I would be more respectful of spooky old legends from now on. I'd learned my lesson.

Rawhead Bloodybones

SEVIER COUNTY

We'd been running around Mamaw's yard all day long, playing in the creek, chasing each other through the apple orchard, and messing around catching fireflies till us kids were all worn out. We were sniping at each other all through supper, so Mamaw gathered us around the fireplace as dusk crept up to the windows and said she'd tell us a story.

RAWHEAD BLOODYBONES

Mamaw told the best stories of anyone in the wide world, but we had a favorite, and all of us started clamoring for it. "Tell us about Rawhead," I exclaimed.

"Rawhead Bloodybones," my littlest brother agreed. It was a big sentence for someone his age. I was impressed he remembered it. Of course it was the kind of tale a kid will remember for a long time, preferably safe under the covers in their bed.

Outside the house, the wind picked up and set the tree branches to scratching against the roof. The sound made us jump every time because we thought it was Rawhead sneaking up on us while we were around the fire. It set the mood for the story Mamaw told us that night.

"Rawhead Bloodybones has been around for a good long while," she began.

Rawhead Bloodybones was one of the many devils that haunt the world. He's always waiting for unsuspecting souls to walk near his hiding place so he can grab them and drag them away. Folks have been seeing this creature and his evil brothers for many years. Whenever a Rawhead comes to a town or village, folks sing the old song as a warning.

Rawhead and Bloody Bones
Steals the wrong 'uns from their homes.
Takes them to his dirty den,
And they are never seen again.

Like the old song says, Rawhead Bloodybones was drawn to evildoers and mischief-makers, killers and gossips, thieves and naughty children. He sensed the mischief in them, and he'd come looking for them when dusky dark came around each night.

Now in these parts, we didn't have any Rawhead Bloodybones for a good while. Then a new couple moved into the settlement who were terrible gossips. They'd find out every bad thing you ever said and every bad choice you ever made, and they'd tell folks in the settlement all about it. They'd harp on your supposed crimes until you were red hot with embarrassment and felt inclined to make another bad choice, this time involving those terrible gossips. You couldn't scratch a fly away from your nose in Sunday school without them telling your mama that you were wiggling about and not listening to the teacher.

Folks asked the preacher to speak to them, but they wouldn't listen. They thought they were doing God's work for him, keeping the people in the settlement in line. Nothing anyone said to them would change their mind. In fact, the men and women who talked to them about it became their worst victims.

And that's what did them in the end. They accused one of the granny women living in the hills nearby of being an evil witch. They said they saw a black cat crossing their yard one night and then running up the path that led to the granny woman's house, and they knew it was old Lizzie sneaking around spying on folks.

No one in the settlement believed that story. Everyone went to old Lizzie for simples to heal their ailments since the doctor lived so far off. Folks in town thought she was an angel sent from God to take care of them. But there was a grain of truth to the story. Old Lizzie was descended from witches; only she used good magic to heal folks when the herbal remedies weren't working.

Old Lizzie didn't want to be driven away from her home by those two gossips. She decided they'd done enough damage in the settlement, so she used a spell taught to her by her granny to call up Rawhead Bloodybones to deal with them. She lit several candles and put them around a picture she drew of the evil spirit. Then she began to chant: "Rawhead and Bloodybones. Rawhead and Bloodybones." The light from the windows disappeared as if the sun had been snuffed out like a candle. Dark clouds billowed into the clearing, and the howl of dark spirits could be heard in the wind that pummeled the treetops. Then a bolt of silver lightning left the plate and streaked out through the window, heading into the woods. It drove deep into the mountainside, down to the place where one of the evil spirits was sleeping.

When the silver light struck the evil spirit, it woke up and flew up to the mountaintop to look around. It was a long time since it had been out and about in the world, and it didn't have a solid form no more. So it swept down to a cabin in the woods where they'd slaughtered some hogs and grabbed a skinned boar's head that was lying about, claiming it for its own.

Now that it had a head, the evil spirit could speak. It called out: "Bloody bones, get up and dance!" Immediately, a heap of bones left behind by the slaughtering of the pigs reassembled themselves until they formed the skeleton of a big old boar hog walking upright. The spirit placed the boar's skinned head atop the bony skeleton, and Rawhead Bloodybones had himself a new body.

Rawhead Bloodybones went searching through the woods for weapons to use against the two gossips that were plaguing old Lizzie. He borrowed the sharp teeth of a dying panther, the claws of a long-dead bear, and the tail from a rotting raccoon and put them over his skinned head and bloody bones.

Then Rawhead Bloodybones went down into the holler, looking for the couple who were making so much trouble for folks in the settlement. He slipped into the barn where the couple kept their horse and wagon and climbed up into the loft and waited for the two gossips to come home.

It was dusk when the gossiping couple came home. The husband drove the wagon into the barn and unhitched the horse. The horse snorted in fear, sensing the presence of Rawhead Bloodybones in the loft. Wondering what was disturbing his usually calm animal, the husband looked around and saw a large pair of eyes staring down at him from the darkness above.

The husband was cumfluttered at the sight. He frowned, thinking it was one of the local kids fooling around in his barn. "What in tarnation have you got those big eyes fer?" he snapped, thinking the kids were trying to scare him with some crazy mask.

"To see your grave," Rawhead Bloodybones whispered softly.

The husband snorted irritably and put his horse into the stall.

When he came out, he saw Rawhead Bloodybones leaning out of the loft so that his luminous yellow eyes and big bear claws could clearly be seen.

"What have you got those big claws fer?" he snapped. "You look ridiculous."

"To dig your grave," Rawhead intoned softly, his voice a deep rumble that raised the hairs on the back of the husband's neck. He stirred uneasily, not sure how the crazy kid in his loft could have made such a scary sound.

He hurried to the door and let himself out of the barn. Rawhead Bloodybones slipped out of the loft and climbed down the side of the barn behind him. With nary a rustle, Rawhead Bloodybones raced through the field and up the path to a large, moonlit oak tree. He hid in the shadow of the tree so that the only things showing were his gleaming yellow eyes, his bear claws, and his raccoon tail.

When the husband came level with the oak tree on the side of the path, he gave a startled yelp. Staring at Rawhead Bloodybones, he gasped: "You nearly knocked the heart right out of me! What have you got that crazy tail fer?"

"To sweep your grave," Rawhead Bloodybones boomed, his enchanted voice echoing through the field, getting louder and louder with each echo.

Afeared for his life, the gossiping husband took to his heels and ran for his cabin, screaming at the top of his lungs. He raced past the old well house, past the woodpile, over the rotting fence, and into his yard. Just as her husband reached the porch, his wife came out the front door to see what was wrong.

At once, Rawhead Bloodybones was there, looming out of the shadows to face the gossiping couple who made so much trouble for folks in the settlement. The couple stared in terror at Rawhead Bloodybones' gleaming yellow eyes, at his bloody bone skeleton with its long bear claws, sweeping raccoon's tail, and razor-sharp panther teeth.

"What in tarnation have you got those big teeth fer?" the husband gasped desperately, clutching at his wife in terror.

"To eat you up!" Rawhead Bloodybones roared, descending on the gossiping couple. They screamed—one good long wail of terror in the dark night. Then there was nothing but silence, and the sound of crunching.

"Nothing more was ever seen or heard of the gossiping couple after that night," Mamaw concluded her tale. "But Rawhead Bloodybones, he is still loose in these here mountains, searching for folks that aren't doing right by their neighbors. Whenever he senses mischief, Rawhead Bloodybones comes looking for the people that done it, just as soon as the dusky dark comes to the holler."

"What does he do then?" I asked, wide-eyed. All us kids were huddled together in a bunch by the fire, clinging to one another because we were so scared.

"You don't want to know," Mamaw said solemnly. "Now go to bed."

We gulped, then did what Mamaw told us. We were shivering and shaking as we all crawled under the covers. I prayed that no one would need the privy in the middle of the night, cause none of us were moving out of that bed. We didn't want to meet up with old Rawhead Bloodybones lurking down in the holler. No how.

Resources

"A Ghost Train." 1896. *The Nashville American*, Nashville, TN, February 6.

"A Hairy Ghost. Grewsome Tale of a Traveler Who Had Been Strangled in Bed." 1895. *Knoxville Journal*, Knoxville, TN, January 25.

"A Haunted Court House. Restless Spooks in a Tennessee County Building." 1889. *Bismarck Tribune*, Bismarck, ND, April 7.

"A True Story of a Ghost, and Conjugal Fidelity." 1820. *Clarksville Gazette*, Clarksville, TN, May 20.

Andrew Jackson Foundation. 2018. *Andrew Jackson's Hermitage: Official Guidebook*. Nashville, TN: Beckon Books.

Appalachian Magazine. 2018. *Mountain Superstitions, Ghost Stories & Haint Tales*. Charleston, WV: Stately Ties Media.

Arneach, Lloyd. 2008. *Long-Ago Stories of the Eastern Cherokee*. Charleston, SC: The History Press.

Arntz, Sarah. 2018. "Worst Train Accident in U.S. History." In *Nashville Public Library*. https://library.nashville.org/blog/2018/07/worst-train-accident-us-history.

Anderson, Geneva. 1939. "Tennessee Tall Tales." *Tennessee Folklore Society Bulletin* 5, no. 3.

Asfar, Dan. 2004. *Haunted Battlefields*. Auburn, WA: Lone Pine Publishing.

Asfar, Dan, and Edrick Thay. 2003. *Ghost Stories of the Civil War*. Auburn, WA: Lone Pine Publishing.

Aswell, James R., et al. 1940. *God Bless the Devil: Liar's Bench Tales*. Chapel Hill: The University of North Carolina Press.

Baldwin, Juanitta. 2005. *Smoky Mountain Ghostlore*. Kodak, TN: Suntop Press.

———. 2011. *Smoky Mountain Stories*. Kodak, TN: Suntop Press.

———. 2007. *Smoky Mountain Tales*, vol. 1. Kodak, TN: Suntop Press.

———. 2008. *Smoky Mountain Tales*, vol. 2. Kodak, TN: Suntop Press.

Baliya, Erin. 2022. "From the Inside: The Great Train Wreck of 1918, the Country's Worst Train Disaster." In *Citrus County Chronicle*. https://www.chronicleonline.com/from-the-inside-the-great -train-wreck-of-1918-the-country-s-worst-train-disaster/article _7285b901-2d0c-5948-903b-23ffeb2306d6.html.

Barefoot, Daniel W. 2002. *Haints of the Hills*. Winston-Salem, NC: John F. Blair, Publisher.

Battle, Kemp P. 1986. *Great American Folklore*. New York: Doubleday.

Bolton, W. Lewis. 2015. *Smoky Mountain Jack Tales of Winter and Old Christmas*. Bloomington, IN: Xlibris.

Botkin, B. A., ed. 1944. *A Treasury of American Folklore*. New York: Crown Publishers.

———. 1949. *A Treasury of Southern Folklore*. New York: Crown Publishers.

Brewer, J. Mason. 1972. *American Negro Folklore*. Chicago: Quadrangle Books.

Brown, Alan. 2009. *Haunted Tennessee*. Mechanicsburg, PA: Stackpole Books.

———. 2004. *Stories from the Haunted South*. Jackson: University of Mississippi Press.

Brown, John N. 2002. "History of the Bell Witch." In *Ghosts & Spirits of Tennessee*. http//johnsrealmonline.com/paranormal/bellwitch/ adams.

Brown, John N., ed. 2003. "Wampus Cat Encounter." In *Ghosts & Spirits of Tennessee*. http//johnsrealmonline.com/paranormal/ submitted/page-03.html.

Chase, Richard. 1948. *Grandfather Tales*. New York: Houghton Mifflin Company.

Childs, Alice. 1929. *American Speech* 5, No. 2. Baltimore: Williams & Wilkins Company.

Coffin, T. P., and H. Cohen. 1966. *Folklore in America*. New York: Doubleday and AMP.

———. 1973. *Folklore from the Working Folk of America*. New York: Anchor Press/Doubleday.

Coggins, Allen R. "Dutchman's Grade Railway Accident." In *Tennessee Encyclopedia*. https://tennesseeencyclopedia.net/entries /dutchmans-grade-railway-accident.

Cohen, Daniel, and Susan Cohen. 2002. *Hauntings and Horrors*. New York: Dutton Children's Books.

Coleman, Christopher K. 2011. *Ghosts and Haunts of Tennessee*. Winston-Salem, NC: John F. Blair, Publisher.

———. 1999. *Ghosts and Haunts of the Civil War*. Nashville, TN: Rutledge Hill Press.

Cox, John Harrington. 1934. "Negro Tales from West Virginia." *Journal of American Folklore* 47, no. 186.

Cunningham, Laura. 2009. *Haunted Memphis*. Charleston, SC: The History Press.

Davis, Donald. 1992. *Southern Jack Tales*. Atlanta, GA: August House, Inc.

Dinan, Kim. 2018. "Mothman and the Flatwoods Monster: Bigfoot, Brown Mountain Lights, and the Bell Witch." In *Blue Ridge Outdoors*. https://www.blueridgeoutdoors.com/features/appalachian -legends.

Dorson, R. M. 1973. *America in Legend*. New York: Pantheon Books.

Duncan, Barbara R., ed. 1998. *Living Stories of the Cherokee*. Chapel Hill: The University of North Carolina Press.

———. 2008. *The Origin of the Milky Way & Other Living Stories of the Cherokee*. Chapel Hill: The University of North Carolina Press.

Editors of *Life*. 1961. *The Treasury of American Folklore*. New York: Time.

Flanagan, J. T., and A. P. Hudson. 1958. *The American Folk Reader*. New York: A. S. Barnes.

Foxfire Students. 2011. *Boogers, Witches, and Haints: Appalachian Ghost Stories*. New York: Anchor Books, 2011.

Gainer, Patrick W. 2008. *Witches, Ghosts and Signs: Folklore of the Southern Appalachians*. Morgantown: West Virginia University Press.

"Ghost Stories." 1894. *The Plain Dealer*, Cleveland, OH, December 16.

Graceland: The Home of Elvis Presley. 2017. "Elvis Presley's Graceland at 35." https://www.graceland.com/blog/posts/elvis-presleys-graceland-at-35.

Guy, Joe. 2008. *The Hidden History of East Tennessee*. Charleston, SC: The History Press.

———. 2011. *The Hidden History of Southeast Tennessee*. Charleston, SC: The History Press.

Hall, Joseph S. 1960. *Smoky Mountain Folks and Their Lore*. Asheville, NC: Gilbert Printing Co. Published in Cooperation with Great Smoky Mountains Natural History Association.

———. 1978. *Yarns and Tales from the Great Smokies*. Asheville, NC: The Cataloochee Press.

Harris, Frankie, and Kim Meredith Harris. 2009. *Haunted Nashville*. Atglen, PA: Schiffer Publishing Ltd.

Hauck, Dennis William. 1996. *Haunted Places: The National Directory*. New York: Penguin Books.

Historic Bell Witch Cave. *History & Legend*. https://www.bellwitchcave.com.

History.com Editors. 2009. "Future President Andrew Jackson Kills Charles Dickinson in a Duel." In *HISTORY*. https://www.history.com/this-day-in-history/andrew-jackson-kills-charles-dickinson-in-duel.

Hosey, Bart. "Nights with Ghosts. The Hen House Hant." 1894. *Knoxville Journal*, Knoxville, TN, November 11.

———. "Nights with Ghosts. The Lost Head." 1894. *Knoxville Journal*, Knoxville, TN, November 4.

———. "Nights with Ghosts. The White Lady of the Great Oak." 1894. *Knoxville Journal*, Knoxville, TN, July 29.

Hudson, Arthur Palmer, and Pete Kyle McCarter. 1934. "The Bell Witch of Tennessee and Mississippi." In *Journal of American Folklore* 47, no. 183.

Huskey, James L. 1956. "The Haunted Church House, and Some Tall Tales." [Transcript of audio interview by Joseph Sargent Hall.] *Joseph Sargent Hall Collection, 1937–1973.* Archives of Appalachia (Box 6, Series I-IB). Johnson City: Eastern Tennessee State University.

Ingram, Martin Van Buren, 1894. *An Authenticated History of the Famous Bell Witch.* http://bellwitch02.tripod.com.

"Juba and the Ghost. By Elizabeth M. Gilmer." 1889. *New Haven Register*, New Haven, CT. January 31.

Kazek, Kelly. 2011. *Forgotten Tales of Tennessee.* Charleston, SC: The History Press.

Kotarski, Georgiana. 2006. *Ghosts of the Southern Tennessee Valley.* Winston-Salem, NC: John F. Blair.

Leach, M. 1958. *The Rainbow Book of American Folk Tales and Legends.* New York: World Publishing.

Mathes, Hodge. 1991. *Tall Tales from Old Smoky.* Johnson City, TN: The Overmountain Press.

"MHC Invites Public to Charles Dickinson Reburial." 2010. *Mid-TN Today.* http://www.midtntoday.com/2010/06/mhc-invites-public -to-charles-dickinson.html.

Middler, Harriet Parks. 1930. *The Bell Witch of Middle Tennessee.* Clarksville, TN: Leaf Chronicle Publishing Co.

Morris, Jeff, Donna Marsh, and Garett Merk. 2011. *Nashville Haunted Handbook.* Cincinnati, OH: Clerisy Press.

Mott, A. S. 2003. *Ghost Stories of America*, vol. II. Edmonton, AB: Ghost House Books.

Norton, Terry L. 2014. *Cherokee Myths and Legends: Thirty Tales Retold.* Jefferson, NC: McFarland & Company, Inc.

O'Rear, Jim. 2009. *Tennessee Ghosts.* Atglen, PA: Schiffer Publishing, Ltd.

Odum, Howard W. 1931. *Cold Blue Moon, Black Ulysses Afar Off.* Indianapolis, IN: Bobbs-Merrill.

Ogle, William. 2015. *Ghosts of Gatlinburg.* Gatlinburg, TN: Self-published.

Olson, Ted, and Anthony P. Cavender, eds. 2009. *A Tennessee Folklore Sampler*. Knoxville: University of Tennessee Press.

PageWise Inc. 2002. *The Legend of the Wampus Cat*. http://ksks .essortment.com/wampuscat_rvmr.htm.

Polley, J., ed. 1978. *American Folklore and Legend*. New York: Reader's Digest Association.

Poore, Tammy J. *Ghost Tales & Superstitions of Southern Appalachian Mountains*. Knoxville, TN: Nine Lives Publishing, 2009.

Price, Charles Edwin. 1992. *Haints, Witches, and Boogers: Tales from Upper East Tennessee*. Winston-Salem, NC: John F. Blair, Publisher.

———. 1995. *Haunted Tennessee*. Johnson City, TN: The Overmountain Press.

———. *The Infamous Bell Witch of Tennessee*. http://www.invink.com /x319.html.

———. 2003. "Is the Bell Witch Watching?" In *Linda Linn's Kentucky Home and Ghost Stories*. http://members.tripod.com/~lindaluelinn /index-57.html.

Prock, Tabitha. 2011. *These Haunted Hills*. Kindle edition. Self-published: CreateSpace Independent Publishing Platform.

Rivers, Michael. 2012. *Appalachia Mountain Folklore*. Atglen, PA: Schiffer Publishing, Ltd.

Roberts, Nancy. 1988. *Ghosts of the Southern Mountains and Appalachia*. Columbia: University of South Carolina Press.

———. 1988. *The Haunted South*. Columbia: University of South Carolina Press.

Russel, Randy, and Janet Barnett. 1999. *The Granny Curse and other Ghosts and Legends from East Tennessee*. Winston-Salem, NC: John F. Blair, Publisher.

Sawyer, Susan. 2013. *Myths and Mysteries of Tennessee*. Guilford, CT: Globe Pequot Press.

Schwartz, Alvin. 1981. *Scary Stories to Tell in the Dark*. New York: HarperCollins.

Simmons, Shane S. 2016. *Legends & Lore of East Tennessee*. Charleston, SC: History Press.

Sircy, Allen. 2020. *Southern Ghost Stories: Murfreesboro Spirits of Stone River*. Self-published: Kindle eBook.

"Skinned Tom." Scaryforkids.com. https://www.scaryforkids.com/skinned-tom.

Skinner, Charles M. 1903. *American Myths and Legends*, vol. 1. Philadelphia: J. B. Lippincott.

———. 1896. *Myths and Legends of Our Own Land*, vols. 1–2. Philadelphia: J. B. Lippincott.

Slimp, Kevin, ed. 2017. *Ghostly Places: A Collection of Chilling Stories about Haunted Places from the Newspapers of Tennessee*. Knoxville, TN: Market Square Publishing.

Still, Laura. 2014. *A Haunted History of Knoxville*. Asheville, NC: Stony River Media.

Thay, Edrick. 2003. *Ghost Stories of the Old South*. Auburn, WA: Ghost House Books.

"The Cabman's Ghost." 1912. *Evening News*, San Jose, CA, June 25.

Traylor, Ken, and Delas M. House Jr. 2007. *Nashville Ghosts and Legends*. Charleston, SC: Haunted America.

"Unveiled by Ghosts: How a Tennessee Mystery Was Explained: Thrilling Story Told About a Haunted House." 1895. *Kalamazoo Gazette*, Kalamazoo, MI, December 19.

Ward, Marshall. 1969. "Marshall Ward: Miles Ward Ghost Story" [audio interview]. *Thomas G. Burton-Ambrose N. Manning Collection, 1899–1989*. Archives of Appalachia (Audiotape 55, Series 8). Johnson City: Eastern Tennessee State University.

Wells, R. W. 2020. *Legend of the Wampus Cat*. Monee, IL: Self-published.

Wigginton, Eliot, ed., and his students. 1973. *Foxfire 2*. New York: Anchor Books.

Windham, Kathryn Tucker. 2016. *Thirteen Tennessee Ghosts and Jeffrey*. Tuscaloosa: The University of Alabama Press.

Young, Richard, and Judy Dockery Young. 1990. *Favorite Scary Stories of American Children*. Atlanta, GA: August House, Inc.

———. 1991. *Ghost Stories from the American Southwest*. Little Rock, AR: August House, Inc.

About the Author

S. E. Schlosser has been telling stories since she was a child, when games of "let's pretend" quickly built themselves into full-length stories acted out with friends. A graduate of Houghton College, the Institute of Children's Literature, and Rutgers University, she created

and maintains the website AmericanFolklore.net, where she shares a wealth of stories from all fifty states, some dating back to the origins of America. Sandy spends much of her time answering questions from visitors to the site. Many of her favorite emails come from other folklorists who delight in practicing the old tradition of who can tell the tallest tale.

About the Illustrator

Artist **Paul G. Hoffman** trained in painting and printmaking. His first extensive illustration work on assignment was in Egypt, drawing ancient wall reliefs for the University of Chicago. His work graces books of many genres—including children's titles, textbooks, short story collections, natural history volumes, and numerous cookbooks. For *Spooky Tennessee* he employed a scratchboard technique and an active imagination.

Printed in the USA
CPSIA information can be obtained
at www.ICGtesting.com
CBHW071110210524
8848CB00006B/11